What
BRASS BANDS
did for me

CHRIS HELME

The History Press

Ransome and Marles Works Band championship-winning quartet, c. 1969. From left to right: Ken Johnson, Robert Oughton, David Aspinall (conductor), Geoffrey Tomlinson and Tommy Hinson.

First published 2009

The History Press
The Mill, Brimscombe Port
Stroud, Gloucestershire, GL5 2QG
www.thehistorypress.co.uk

British Library Cataloguing in Publication Data.
A catalogue record for this book is available from the British Library.

ISBN 978 0 7524 4982 1

Typesetting and origination by The History Press
Printed in Great Britain

CONTENTS

ACKNOWLEDGEMENTS

I would like to take this opportunity to thank all those musicians, conductors and band administrators for all the help and support they have given during the preparation of my book. In addition, I would like to thank all those people who have been delighted to share and send me memories about many of the individual personalities in this book.

I would like to send a special thanks to the following people for all the help, support and encouragement that they have given me during the preparation and very extensive research I have carried out for this publication:

Robert (Bob) Wray; Peter Wilson; W. Bram Thompson; Derek Garside; Geoffrey Brand; Campbell Holmes; Derek Roebuck; Cliff Lack; James Scott; Steve Cooke; David Horsfield; David Pratt; William (Bill) Geldard; Stanley Keen; Ms Joy Carter; Boobs and Brass (Northampton's only all-female brass band); Howard Snell; Jef Sparkes; the committee of the Oxted Band for use of two special band photographs; Daren Blake; Martin Obermuller; www.4barsrest.com; Steve and Linda (*née* Muscroft) Jarvis; Ms Sheelagh Pearson; Richard Grantham; Hugh Johnstone MBE; Ken Johnson; Todmorden Orchestra; Mrs Jill Walsh; Mrs Margaret Midgley; George Bamfitt; Alan Lawton; Charley Brighton, Bram Wiggins; Geoffrey Whitham; John Slinger; John Clay; Denzil Stephens; Frank Mathison; Jeffrey Turner; Brian Minear; Mrs Lorna Williams; Philip Hunt; Clive Donaghue and the Royston Photographic Society; Stuart Atkins; Dr Kenneth Downie; Dr Stephen Bulla; Walter Roberts; Roy Roe; Derek Mitchell; Hemel Hempstead Band, for use of a John Dickinson Band photograph; Dr Roy Newsome; Ronald Helme, for his proof reading and Gavin Holman for the use of images from his website, www.ibew.co.uk

Finally, I would like to thank all those who have allowed me to tell their individual stories; without your help and co-operation this book would not have been possible. In addition, I would to thank the families of those individuals who appear in the book that have passed away. Through this book their memory and musical contribution will live on.

INTRODUCTION

To the insider, the world of brass bands can conjure up all kinds of memories. These can often be from a concert or a contest performance that was played by either a present-day band, or a band that, sadly, has now been confined to the annals of brass band history.

This world of brass bands seems to have had, although some may say to a lesser degree these days, its own unique kind of people. I suppose to use the modern jargon we should call them 'personalities', but in 'banding' circles, whether they are dead or alive, these people are often referred to as 'characters' – and in some cases even elevated to the status of being a 'legend'.

They are people who have produced, time after time, what can only be described as truly magical musical moments in a performance, or perhaps someone with his or her own particular turns of phrase. With that once-in-a-lifetime individual performance of musical brilliance, that unforgettable composition or an arrangement of a piece that will live on forever.

These, of course, include composers, conductors (or should we say bandmasters or musical directors), and the individual players. Many have come from modest musical beginnings and have then grown into household names in this world of brass bands and, in some cases, the wider musical world.

I have been associated with brass bands for almost fifty years, but it was only a little over fifteen years ago that I began my interest in brass band research. I began to wonder where these great performers and characters of yesteryear were today; who are these composers and arrangers whose name you can find in the top left- or top right-hand corners of a piece of music?

Sadly, I discovered that in a number of cases time had taken its toll – but even so, there are few words and publications about their lives, deeds and the lasting memories they have left us. Yes, there are some, but only a few; let us hope in the future we see more, so as to remind us all of these now almost forgotten legends of the past.

So now read on and take a trip with me down memory lane. I hope that once you have read my contribution to the small but growing list of brass band books, publications and articles. I will have re-kindled some of your own memories whether as a player, former playing member of a band, a conductor or one of the invaluable 'backroom doers' that every band needs – yes, and not forgetting the members of that all-important audience. Then this book will act as a reminder or be an insight into the lives of some of those people who can proudly say, 'Look what brass bands did for me ...'

Chris Helme, BEM
enquiries@chrishelme-brighouse.org.uk

(Musical Director, Parks Department - MR. WALTER REYNOLDS)

Programme of Music

To be performed by

ST. HILDA'S BAND

Conductor: Mr. FRANK WRIGHT, L.A.B., R.A.M., R.C.M.

1	MARCH	"Tannhauser"		*Wagner*
2	OVERTURE	"1812"		*Tschaikowsky*
3	SELECTION	"Oberon"		*Weber, arr. Owen*
4	XYLOPHONE SOLO	"Sparks"		*Alford*

Soloist—HARRY RANDOLF

5	EXCERPTS from	"Cavalcade"		*Noel Coward*
6	TROMBONE SOLO	"The Trumpeter"		*Dix*

Soloist—WILLIAM BLACKETT

INTERVAL.

7	HUNGARIAN RHAPSODY, No. 2		*Liszt*
8	TENOR VOCALIST (Song and Chorus)		
	(a) "Our River Thames"	... *arr. Jewell Hennessy*	
	(b) "Irish Folk Song"		*Wright*
9	FUGUE	"St. Anne" ... *Bach, arr. W. Reynolds*	
10	DESCRIPTIVE FANTASIA ... "A Sailor's Life"		*Cope*
11	INTERMEZZO ... "The Grasshopper's Dance"		*Bucalossi*
12	CHORUS	"Hallelujah"	*Handel*

"Trumpet Fanfare"

GOD SAVE THE KING.

Programme   **One Penny**

Holders of a daily chair ticket are entitled to the use of a vacant chair inside the Band enclosure at such times as Mr. M. W. SHANLY has control of the chairs. This privilege does not apply to Brockwell or Finsbury Parks.

All complaints re Chairs and Programmes used at this Band Performance, also enquiries re Chair Season Tickets for L.C.C. Parks and Open Spaces and Royal Parks (price 10/- inclusive); hire or purchase of any class of Garden Chairs should be addressed to—

M. W. SHANLY, 35, King Henry's Road,
South Hampstead, London, N.W.3.

Catalogues sent free on application.

E.--5.   W. Austin & Sons, Printers. Chelsea, S.W. 3.

St Hilda's Band Programme of Music, c. 1934, conducted that season by Frank Wright (see page 114).

1
END CHAIR
PLAYERS

Twenty-three-year-old Ceres Jackson was described as a classy and artistic player. He joined Black Dyke Mills Band in October 1901 as sub-principal cornet to the legendary John Paley. He finally took the 'end chair' position in his own right in 1902.

WILLIE BARR
'The Flying Scot'

Willie Barr will be remembered by many older readers as one of the finest and most frequently heard cornet soloists on the radio during the 1950s and '60s. My own recollection of this brass band legend from north of the border was when I first heard one of his solo performances of Gregor J. Grant's composition, *The Flying Scot*, on a 1967 Scottish CWS recording.

Willie was the eldest son of William (who was also known as Willie, Snr) and Meg Barr. Their two younger sons, James and Lex, and daughter, Bunty, did not follow what had become a family tradition of learning to play a brass instrument. Willie, however, followed in the footsteps of not only his father, but five uncles as well – Jim, Louis, Alex, Charlie and George – who were all instrumentalists in their own right. In fact, the family's brass band connections go back even further, to the days when Willie's grandfather, John Barr, was a founding member and conductor of the Creetown Silver Band near Galloway, during the 1880s.

Willie (jnr) was born in 1926 in Glasgow and began playing at the age of eleven. His father, who was a cornet player with the Scottish CWS Band at the time, gave him his early tuition.

His introduction to playing with a band was when he joined the local Boys' Brigade, and not long after he joined the Glasgow Corporation Gas Department Band under their conductor Herbert Bennett.

During the summer concert season of 1940 young Willie featured regularly as a boy soloist with the Glasgow Corporation Gas Department Band. He had now moved on from receiving tuition from his father to having more advanced lessons from Ben Thornton, principal cornet at Scottish CWS.

In 1941, Willie, then aged fourteen, finally achieved his boyhood ambition by following in his father's footsteps and becoming a member of the Scottish CWS Band. As a boy, he was very enthusiastic, with most of his leisure time being spent at home practicing and listening to recordings of the many fine players of that era.

From the age of fourteen, until he was called-up into the army at eighteen, he was content to remain in the back row cornet section, and always said this was a wise policy, as many promising young players often fail through being promoted before having had a chance to develop naturally.

During the latter part of the Second World War he saw active service. He was wounded whilst serving with the Black Watch, and did not play for over two and a half years. Fortunately, he was transferred to the Royal Norfolk Regiment soon after the war and spent the remaining year of his army service on tour in Germany as the solo cornet of the regimental band.

On his demobilisation in the autumn of 1947, he went into the first cornet section of the Scottish CWS, who were then in the process of re-organising after the war years. In early 1949, Alex Mortimer was appointed the musical director, who then appointed Willie Barr as the band's principal.

With the Scottish CWS Band, he was a familiar face at the National Finals in London, where the band's highest placing came in 1958 when under the baton of William Crozier. Playing Edmund Rubbra's test piece, *Variations on the Shining River*, No. 16, the band was awarded second place behind Foden's Motor Works Band.

Now firmly established as a player of distinction and quickly making a name in solo competitions, Willie was attracting the attention of the foremost English bands of the time.

Willie Barr in 1950 – one of the finest cornet players of his generation.

He was the record winner of the Glasgow and West of Scotland Solo Championship until he stopped entering the event, while still in his early thirties. He won the Scottish Solo Championships in 1948/1949, and was usually the highest placed cornet in the initial entry of qualifiers.

Twice during the 1950s he was invited to take the 'end chair' at Black Dyke Mills Band, but because of the more attractive location (Oxford) he chose instead to accept an invitation from Harry Mortimer to join his Morris Motors Band as leader in 1950. He led the band to success in several contests and very many broadcasts for over a year before being tempted to return to the Scottish CWS Band, with the additional appointment of secretary.

He was secretary of the band for sixteen years until he relinquished the position in 1966/67 to take up a position as teacher of brass instruments with the Edinburgh Education Authority.

On reaching the age of fifty in 1976, Willie found the constant travelling to Glasgow and back several times a week rather tiresome, on top of his daily teaching commitments in Edinburgh. After twenty-three years' service, except between 1950 and 1951 when he was the principal cornet with Morris Motors Band, he retired from the Scottish CWS Band. His next ten years was spent assisting the Royal Scots TA Band, a role which took him all over the country. This included taking part in the Kneller Hall inspections.

William (Willie) Crozier conducts Scottish CWS Band at a rehearsal prior to the 1958 National Brass Band Championships.

Members of the Scottish CWS Band in 1958 on their way to take part in the National Brass Band Championships. The band was conducted by William Crozier, and placed second behind the new National Champions, Foden's Motor Works Band and its conductor Rex Mortimer.

My first encounter with Willie Barr was when my father took me to my first solo contest. One abiding memory of that wintry afternoon in a draughty, dingy Glasgow concert hall is of the stylish cornet player whose sound, technical wizardry and expressive phrasing set him in a different league from the other competitors.

Some years later, I was Willie's opposite number in the Scottish CWS Band. From the principal euphonium chair, I was to learn much more about this 'Flying Scotsman' (as composer Gregor J. Grant dubbed him in a popular cornet feature of the time).

Looking back, now over fifty years, it was primarily the man's glorious sound that impressed most. His heart-warming vibrato and ability to shape a phrase could move one to tears, especially in the traditional Scottish melodies that featured often in our programmes at that time. I have never heard the introduction to the final movement of Howells' *Pageantry* played to better effect by anybody.

Willie was band secretary, and his efficient administration created the best-organised band I'd ever come across. He left nothing to chance, and his meticulous attention to detail bred a sense of security that spilled over into the band's performances.

He had high musical standards and expected the same from those around him. An occasional exchange of glances and hint of a smile meant he approved of what you had just done. Players both young and old cowered at the scowl he would throw around the bandroom at wrong notes and careless entries, even when sight-reading a new piece.

As a new boy, I was never really in his social circle, but in later years, when I took up conducting, he was supportive and encouraging. I remain glad to have played alongside him for those golden years in Scottish Co-op history.

Peter Wilson, principal euphonium SCWS from 1957-1961, then conductor of the Kirkintilloch Band; organising secretary, National Brass Band Championships of Great Britain, 1971-1976; editor of *British Bandsman* from 1977-2001

One of his most popular solos from his long repertoire heard on his many radio broadcasts and concert solo performances was *The Flying Scot*, and was dedicated to him by the composer Gregor J. Grant in appreciation of his playing.

Over the years, Willie played under many conductors, including: Sir Malcolm Sargent, Sir Adrian Boult, Karl Rankl and Sir Arthur Bliss, amongst the orchestral greats, and too many to recall in the brass band world. While Scottish CWS was considered by many as the graveyard of conductors, Willie found Fred, Harry and Alex Mortimer all inspirational figures to play for; George Hawkins, J.A. Greenwood and many others also demanded a high standard of excellence.

Willie was a member of the first cornet section in Harry Mortimer's 1950s 'All Star Concert Band of Great Britain', and the principal cornet of its Scottish counterpart under Drake Rimmer.

Enoch Jackson, the principal trumpet at the Scottish National Orchestra and Professor of Trumpet at the Scottish Academy of Music, always advised his students to listen to Willie Barr on record for a perfect example of triple-tonguing techniques.

Willie was himself Professor of Cornet at the Dreghorn Military School in Edinburgh for young bandsmen during the 1970s. He continued to teach in Lothian schools until his retirement in 1991.

At his peak, Willie Barr was one of the finest cornet players of his generation, and the few recordings of him that do survive are a testament to some truly first-class playing. He died in 2008.

THE SCOTTISH CO-OP BAND

(RE-NAMED THE CO-OP FUNERAL CARE BAND IN 2009)

The Scottish Co-op Band's first public performance was a far cry from the kind it performs today, whether it is on the concert stage or the contest platform. Fittingly, the band's first musical refrains were heard drifting across the waters of the Firth of Clyde. The date was 1 October 1918, and the occasion was a pleasure cruise to Lochgoilhead, and had been arranged by the directors of the Scottish Co-operative Wholesale Society (SCWS), for soldiers who were recuperating from the wounds they had received during the First World War.

This first performance on the deck of the steamer 'Lord of the Isles' was the culmination of some persistent lobbying by employees from the SCWS. Success came following a series of workforce meetings held in 1917, and a further meeting with the directors when the authorisation to form a band was given. Mr Miller, the manager of the furniture department and a prime mover in lobbying for a band for almost two decades, was often described as the 'father of the band' and was elected as its first president.

It was soon performing many concerts and engagements for and on behalf of the SCWS. The band entered its first contest in the summer of 1919 and won first prize – sadly, it was a prize based on its deportment rather than its skill at playing! At the first contest where playing was the test it came last out of twenty-six bands; there was much still to do.

The members of this early 1950s Scottish CWS Band included: Willie Barr, Gilbert Watts, Jackie Elliott, Derward Brown, Walter Nesbitt, James Megahy, Willie Haddow, James McKee, Bram and Charlie Thompson, Roddy Campbell, Willie McPherson, Peter Wilson, Peter Moore, Robert Nairn, James McMillan, Paul Beck, Robert Arnott, John Arnott, Harry Masters, Bert Masson, Willie Robb, Jimmy Caruthers. Sitting in the middle between the two horn players is the conductor Robert Oughton.

Pictured here in October 1958, Sandy Auld, Tas Carruthers, Bram Thompson, Willie Barr and Peter Wilson listen to a tape recording of their last rehearsal before travelling to the national championship final a few days later.

DEREK GARSIDE

'Arguably the finest player of his generation'

On 22 October 1994, for the first time in more years than I care to remember, I went to a band concert. Not just any concert, mind you, but one of Brighouse and Rastrick's noted annual massed band concerts at Huddersfield Town Hall.

Taking part in what was the fiftieth season of these annual events with B & R was the legendary cornet player Mr Derek M. Garside, one of the finest cornet players of his generation and a man who began his illustrious playing career in his hometown of Brighouse. The first time I saw him perform live as a soloist was in 1967 at the Royal Albert Hall when he was accompanied by his wife Janne Edwards-Garside, ARCM on the piano.

Derek Malcolm Garside was born in 1930, the youngest son of Percy and Florence Garside, and was from a staunchly religious family who were regulars at the Central Methodist Church in Brighouse, where in later years he was to delight audiences with his cornet playing. Music, and particularly singing, would have been familiar sounds in the Garside household, with his father Percy being a noted baritone singer, who performed in many local amateur productions in his younger days and was very much a professional in his later years.

His mother Florence, or 'Flo', as many of her good friends were allowed to call her, was herself a respected local pianist. She died in 1974 and was interred in the family grave at Brighouse Cemetery.

Not long after Derek's ninth birthday, his father asked him what he wanted to learn to play. It was expected that he would play some kind of instrument, just as the rest of the family did. Even today, Derek still cannot recall why he gave the answer he did: it was something he replied on the spur of the moment, without even thinking. 'A trumpet,' he said.

A couple of weeks later he arrived home from school to be greeted by his father, 'There's a case in that corner for you, go and have a look at it.' It wasn't the trumpet he'd asked for but a cornet, something he'd never seen before. 'By the way,' added his father, 'you start having lessons next Friday night with Mr Roberts.' In later years Derek found out that his father's best friend, Arthur Thornton, had arranged with the Brighouse and Rastrick Band to loan him the instrument, and had also arranged his first cornet lessons as well.

Mr Fred J. Roberts was no slouch when it came to playing a cornet: at that time he was the principal cornet player of Brighouse and Rastrick. In the very early 1940s, young Derek had progressed enough to join Clifton and Lightcliffe Band. On the occasions his father was away singing in Blackpool, Arthur would call round to ensure young Derek was practicing, and particularly before he went to his Friday evening lesson.

In 1942 Derek entered his first competition at Shipley near Bradford, but didn't win anything on

This photograph of the CWS (Manchester) Band was taken back stage at the Royal Albert Hall at some point between 1954 and 1959 and shows: Alf Morton, Charles Unsworth, Harold Lang, Derek Garside, Cyril Howarth, Joe Hughes, Sid Poole, Alec Watson, Joe Poole, Joe Swift, Tom White, Arthur Pugh, Jack Watson, Tommy Dowers, Brian Taylor, Lyn Williams, Jim Waggott, Brian Wilkinson, Jack Phillips, Dennis Smith, Bert Howarth, Gordon Higginbottom and Bill Morbey.

that day. A prize wasn't far off though, and on the 30 October 1943, he collected a third prize at a competition in Heckmondwike. A slow melody that he entered at Bradford on the 27 November 1943 not only won first prize in the under-fourteen-year-olds junior section and again in the fourteen- to nineteen-year-old intermediate section, but also won the first prize in the open age section as well. Towards the end of 1943 he re-joined his tutor Fred Roberts, only this time as a player in the cornet section of Brighouse and Rastrick Band.

One of his first major successes with Brighouse and Rastrick came in 1946, a few months after leaving school, when he was the band's repiano player. With Eric Ball as its professional conductor, it won the premier title at the National Brass Band Championships Finals in London, playing Henry Geehl's test piece *Oliver Cromwell*.

After Brighouse and Rastrick took the title Derek was promoted onto the solo cornet bench, playing third man down to Fred Roberts.

In 1947 Fred was offered the position of bandmaster and advisor at the re-organised CWS (Manchester) Band, working alongside its newly appointed professional conductor, Eric Ball.

In December 1947, at the age of seventeen, Derek was invited to be the principal cornet for the CWS (Manchester) Band. Along with every other member of the band he was offered employment with CWS and was a full-time employee in the accounts department until 1969.

Gradually the band was built up around its newly appointed principal solo cornet player. The final piece of the jigsaw was put in place following the appointment of Alex Mortimer as its musical director in 1954.

From the time Derek first joined the CWS (Manchester) Band in 1947 and up to 1970, the band took part in the British Open Championships in the Kings Hall, Belle Vue on eighteen occasions, won it four times, and placed on twelve occasions. The band qualified for the London Finals almost every year, and its success in the North West Finals was unrivalled. The band finally achieved its crowning glory on Saturday 20 October 1962, when at last it became the number one band at the *Daily Herald* National Brass Band Championships at the Royal Albert Hall, with musical director, Alex Mortimer,

Owen Brannigan sings 'The Trumpet Shall Sound' from the Messiah, *while Derek plays the Bach 'D' trumpet and Alex Mortimer conducts the CWS (Manchester) Band. The players are, from right to left, back row: Ian Richards, Harry Cooke, Harold Lang, Colin Waggott, Jack Phillips, -?-, Joe Poole. Front row: Bob Richards, Peter Gill, Hayden Harris, -?-, -?-. This was typical of concerts that the band performed between 1964 and 1968.*

At the CWS in Balloon Street, Manchester in the early 1950s we all knew about Derek Garside and from the vast Accounts Department overlooking Hanover Street we could often hear him practicing with the CWS band over the road. Mostly it was just a cacophony of jumbled notes but occasionally came the crystal clear sweetness of Derek's cornet. Then the windows would be opened, pens would be poised in mid air, and only the office manager would glare from his elevated glass-fronted cubicle. That's the way I remember it – a truly magnificent sound.
Frank Melia (Pudsey), employed at the CWS in Balloon Street, 1951-1970

Between 1965 and 1969 Brian Cronshaw sat next to Derek as the assistant principal cornet player at CWS (Manchester) Band and can recall many happy memories and highlights from those days. 'It was a privilege to have had the opportunity to play assistant to him.'
Derek had been the principal cornet player at the CWS for twenty years and was not only respected throughout the band but throughout the brass band world. His concert, contest and recordings are testament to his outstanding musicianship. I can recall one of many occasions when we shared the contest platform: one of the most memorable was in 1966 at the British Open Championship contest at the Kings Hall, Belle Vue. The test piece was John Ireland's *A Downland Suite* and throughout the whole performance Derek never took a break, a truly fabulous performance by one of the greatest cornet players of his generation. The winners that day? CWS, of course!
Brian Cronshaw, assistant principal cornet CWS (Manchester) Band, 1965-1969

playing Frank Wright's arrangement of Verdi's *Force of Destiny* – an achievement it went on to repeat the following year in 1963 playing *Belmont Variations* by Sir Arthur Bliss.

This long-awaited win was only three months after another important event in Derek's life – his marriage to Janne Edwards, an accomplished pianist in her own right. After their marriage they were to be seen and heard together over many years in concert platforms throughout the British Isles and overseas. Sadly, Janne passed away in 2003.

His outstanding musicianship was recognised by the Worshipful Company of Musicians, who he performed for in 1968. As a freelance trumpet player he performed with all the major provincial professional orchestras. In addition to this his playing of the Bach Trumpet was constantly in demand throughout the North of England. In 1969 Derek was the first recipient of the Insignia of Honour, which was awarded annually to a working instrumentalist who had given conspicuous service to brass bands.

He took part in over 300 radio broadcasts and a number of television programmes. In 1969 he was teaching brass in Manchester schools.

The CWS (Manchester) Band continued to tour extensively throughout the United Kingdom, and went on numerous continental tours, including a visit to Niagara Falls and Toronto in June/July 1972. The tour involved three other bands, Fairey Aviation, Black Dyke Mills and the GUS (Footwear). Sadly, owing to ill health, and to everyone's disappointment, Alex Mortimer was unable to make the trip that summer. His place as conductor was taken by Derek Garside, on what was then his first outing as the band's newly appointed musical director – a daunting task even for someone with Derek's wealth of experience.

In 1973 Derek led the band to qualification at the North West Area contest, ensuring it took part in the National Finals once again. This was a memorable occasion for Derek on what was his first appearance at the Royal Albert Hall as the band's musical director, and he led them to a second place behind Brighouse and Rastrick, playing Hubert Bath's test piece *Freedom*. Under Derek's direction the band did well and was awarded first place in both 1975 and again in 1976 at the North West Area Finals.

During the late seventies Derek was a peripatetic brass teacher in the Bradford schools. The end of April 1979 saw him back in the spotlight when he accepted an offer to become the musical director of Foden's Motor Works Band.

The CWS (Manchester) Band came to an end in 1985. Today, the band's many trophies, prizes and historical records are safely locked away in the vaults of the CWS in Manchester. The band had been a well-respected and admired household name amongst the country's banding fraternity for over eighty years.

In 1988 he was at the London Finals again, this time conducting Llansaint Silver in the fourth section championships with Ray Steadman Allen's test piece, *Wealden Rhapsody*. His return to the Town Hall in Huddersfield in 1996 was to a full house as the guest soloist for Brighouse and Rastrick's celebration concert, and was a fitting venue and tribute for this legend of the brass band movement. It was here at the same venue, half a century earlier, that he first performed as a boy soloist.

Following that appearance at Huddersfield, he accepted an invitation to be a member of a select band of musicians, who were rightly called the 'Kings of Brass'.

In 2001, after seven years, numerous full-house concerts and three CDs, this unique band, made up from many of Derek's contemporaries, and where one of the qualifications was a minimum time served in top flight banding of forty years, played its last concert. Along with Derek they all epitomised the sense of fellowship in banding.

The CWS (Manchester) Band Quartet in 1955. From left to right: Derek Garside, Thomas White, Alex Mortimer (standing), Colin Adamson, Denis Smith.

A TRIP TO NIAGARA FALLS

Maybe it was because Dennis Hinchliffe, President of HMC Travel Advisors Ltd, Niagara Falls was born in Rotherham. Maybe because devotees of the brass band sound who emigrated to Canada over the years were reluctant to cut their links with the traditions of this unique sound. Or it could have been that transatlantic air travel was down to as little as seven hours? Who knows. But the undisputable truth was that in 1972, four of the great brass bands, accompanied by three famous guest conductors went on an unforgettable trip to Niagara Falls between 30 June and 9 July 1972.

The first enquiry about this trip came a year earlier when Geoffrey Brand received a telephone call from one of the directors of the travel company. Preparations were made and when the big day finally came GUS (Footwear), Fairey, CWS (Manchester) and Black Dyke Mills bands boarded the aircraft with hundreds of supporters and headed across the Atlantic Ocean.

Geoffrey Brand commented at the time, 'One day bands will visit every part of the world. The process of modern travel makes it ever more possible, and the process has already made great strides forward. The visit of the four bands to Niagara Falls and the surrounding areas in July is the latest in this progression of cultural contact. Those who are fortunate in being part of the "team" may well be seen in years to come as the forbears of regular transatlantic fraternisation.'

Geoffrey penned those words thirty-eight years ago: little did he know then just how true his words would eventually become.

From left to right: Eric Ball, Derek Garside, Stanley Boddington, Kenneth Dennison, Geoffrey Brand, Roy Newsome and Harry Mortimer.

WILLIAM LANG
'A brass band legend'

The name William Lang – known to his many friends as either Willie or Bill – will instinctively bring to mind one of the brass band world's finest cornet players, and someone who went on to become one of the most respected orchestral trumpet players of his generation.

If you asked the likes of Jim Shepherd, Derek Garside and Maurice Murphy, three cornet players who themselves have been described as 'a class above' most other cornet players of their generation, who they admired and aspired to emulate, I have no doubt they would all mention Willie Lang. You will still hear in the contest bar and tea room discussions about who is or has been the best cornet player, and again the name of Willie Lang would be a firm favourite.

He came from a musical family: his father played the flute and his grandfather a tin whistle. His father, a ship's engineer before Willie was born, always said, 'A person need never be bored if he played a musical instrument.'

Willie was born in 1919 in the hilltop community of Norland, a small village in the old West Riding area that sits at the edge of the Pennines. In those days the family lived quite close to a disused quarry, and it was in a hut at the bottom of this quarry that the Norland Prize Band, the village band, held its weekly rehearsals. During the summer, the band would usually take part in local contests, and if the weather was really nice the band would practice its test piece outside in the bottom of the quarry, and young Willie would spend many hours watching and listening to it.

Before his entry into the world of brass bands he had already mastered the technique of rubber wash-board playing, to such an extent he could quite easily play a chromatic scale.

Three members of the Ferodo Works Band during the mid-1950s. Left to right: Les Holden, soprano cornet; Willie Lang, principal cornet; Campbell Holmes, second trombone.

His initial introduction to a brass instrument came in the form of a bugle which his father gave him; his uncle then taught him to play the army calls. Having mastered them all, he soon became frustrated at not being able to play a complete march. He decided it was time to have a go with a band, and looked no further than over his garden fence.

He was introduced to the band's conductor, George Ramsden, who gave him his first cornet – a great day, Willie remembered. After a few weeks he was so impressed with Willie's playing that he was taken in and signed up as the latest member of the band, and all at the tender age of nine.

By 1930, a year after he joined the band, he entered his first slow melody competition, and with a start of fifty points managed to win. This was the first of many awards he received throughout his long musical career.

Back in those days Norland Prize Band was a local second section band, and every year it entered the Halifax and district band contest. Unfortunately, Willie had joined too late to sign up to take part in that year's contest, but nevertheless the band still let him go along for the experience.

In the world of brass bands, being in the right place at the right time has sometimes been known to pay dividends. In 1932 when the Bradford City Band qualified to play in the national championships at the Crystal Palace it was a cornet player short – and to Willie's surprise he was asked to take the vacant cornet position. The test piece was John Ireland's *A Downland Suite*, a difficult piece for a young cornet player. The Crystal Palace was a wonderful place, with many famous bandsmen; for any young player it was almost magical. He was to come to know many of them personally over the years as his career developed.

It was during this period that Wilfred Swingler joined Bradford City Band and replaced Frank as the principal cornet player. Willie always described Frank Haigh as a wonderful player and someone who made his playing sound so effortless and natural. He was someone who influenced Willie's own playing. Frank Haigh gave Willie one piece of advice that he remembered throughout his own career and considered it good advice for any young player: 'Learn all you can from everyone, but ultimately develop your own style and individuality.'

Willie's philosophy was always quite simple. The best way to improve your own playing standard was by playing amongst better players than yourself, which would then gradually see your own playing improve.

In 1932, Albert Jackson was the 'G' trombone player at the band. During the following year his brother Harold, Black Dyke's principal cornet player, visited the band. Willie always felt that he was one of the finest cornet players he had the privilege of hearing and later playing along side. Harry Grace took the opportunity of asking Harold if he would like to sit in on the rehearsal, but he excused himself by saying he didn't have his instrument with him. Somewhat naively young Willie offered him his as he was anxious to hear him play. Somewhat reluctantly the offer was accepted, and Harold took out his mouth piece from an old leather mouth-piece wallet. Taking the instrument he then sat in Willie's place, second man to Wilf Swingler, who offered to change positions and sit second man to Harold. This was an experience Willie never forgot.

Harry Grace asked him afterwards what he thought of Willie's cornet, Harold promptly replied, 'I don't know how the hell anyone can play on such an instrument.' This proved a good omen for him, because shortly after the band gave Willie a brand new cornet!

Harold Jackson went back to Black Dyke, and made it known he wanted Willie as his assistant. An audition invitation came not long after. It was 1935 when he entered the small band room at Queensbury for the first time, an ordeal he never forgot. This was the first time he met Black Dyke's legendary bandmaster, Mr Arthur O. Pearce. He introduced him to the members of the band, and then asked him to sit next to Harold Jackson. At this point Harold promptly walked out, leaving Willie to get on with it! This, it transpired, was a deliberate ploy.

The Black Dyke Mills Band Quartet won the championship of Great Britain in 1947 and 1948. From left to right: William Lang, solo cornet; Frank Hiley, second cornet; Gordon Sutcliffe, solo horn; and Denzil S. Stephens, euphonium.

He was accepted, and this was the start of Willie's career in first-class banding, playing alongside some of the giants of the brass band world: Harold Jackson principal cornet, Rowland Jones, principal euphonium, Haydn Robinson, principal trombone, Bernard Burns, soprano – a formidable team indeed. Willie moved to the 'end chair' in 1936 after Harold Jackson went to Besses o'th' Barn Band.

Here is Willie's description of the inside of the Black Dyke's bandroom in 1936: 'The seats for players were like milking stools, almost 2ft high, you were neither sitting nor standing. Older members used to say they had been designed so as to discourage players "nodding-off".' They were said to be quite dangerous pieces of furniture, and reputed to have been in use for the about eighty years. The chairs were still in regular use when Harry Mortimer was appointed the professional conductor; he took pity on the players and recommended the company replace them with proper chairs.

Willie soon found it difficult to attend both his evening classes and all the engagements and rehearsals of the band. The band had already moved one of its rehearsal nights for his benefit, an unprecedented move in the band's history. It was therefore mutually agreed that he would leave for the time being, but to keep his hand in he played for a short time with Hebden Bridge Band.

He worked as an apprentice builder and stonemason at Parkers Yard, Sowerby Bridge, and was so good he was paid a tradesman's wage while still a boy. His handiwork can still be seen on the columns of the former Barclays Bank, Sowerby Bridge, near Halifax.

Having been deferred from war duties in 1939, his call up papers finally arrived in 1940. He initially joined the Artillery, but later transferred to the Royal Engineers and went on to serve in North Africa, Italy, Austria, and eventually in Germany, as a tank commander. Willie returned in 1946 and resumed his 'end chair' position at Black Dyke; that was after the obligatory audition for all potential new members. He could still remember feeling nervous as he entered the band room and he felt the emotion welling up as he walked over to his stool.

Throughout his years with Black Dyke the rehearsals always started at 7 p.m. and finished at 9 p.m. Any business took place afterwards. At five minutes to seven there would be possibly only two men there, Arthur O. Pearce and the librarian. Willie often wondered if he had mistaken the night of the rehearsal, yet at three minutes to seven the full band were there sitting down ready to play. The same thing happened at the end of the rehearsal: if there was no business to discuss the place was empty in one minute.

After the war years Willie joined the Black Dyke Quartet along with Alwyn Pinches on cornet, Gordon Sutcliffe on horn and Denzil Stephens playing the euphonium, and for a short time, a very talented young cornetist, Frank Hiley. Joe Wood was its conductor. This was a successful combination.

In 1947 he entered the preliminary solo championships, which were held in Bradford, and that year he played *Weber's Last Waltz*. He deliberately chose that solo because it had a bigger range than many of the usual solos. The contest day arrived but he didn't feel very optimistic about his chances, feeling he had not been back long enough to prepare himself. He met a number of old friends at the contest, including Harry Grace, from his Bradford City Band days. Harry told him to go out there and enjoy himself. He did just that, and won first prize.

That same year, Harry Mortimer was appointed the professional conductor at Black Dyke; his presence put new life into the band. Willie held Harry in high esteem and considered him to be a natural musician with a great gift for getting an overall picture of a piece from a band. He worried about detail, certainly, but never let it sacrifice the overall sound. He always looked supremely confident, which in turn inspired his players with a greater confidence.

There were some wonderful performances, concerts and contests given during that period under HM. Back in those days, however, Willie felt that Belle Vue was never a lucky place for Black Dyke. On one occasion he had a solo to play. Early on in the piece, with a top A natural looming, he felt relaxed – but then, for some unknown reason, he split it. The groans from the audience echoed round the Kings Hall, and from that point on the band simply collapsed. Willie once remarked that it seemed more laughable than tragic, as later in the piece there was a rather difficult cadenza which was played without any problems. However, the band did not recover sufficiently from the earlier mistake to change the eventual contest placing. It was probably the only time in his career with first-class bands where he 'fluffed' on a contest stage.

In 1950 Alex Mortimer had come to Black Dyke to take over as conductor from his brother Harry (the same year the band was barred from the national championships because of its three consecutive wins in 1947, 48 and 49). However, it was back to its winning ways with another first place in 1951.

Willie did not play with Black Dyke at the 1953 finals, because for a short period he played with Brighouse and Rastrick. He enjoyed playing with the band, but he never felt as though he could settle there. In 1954 Willie went back to Black Dyke, although not for long. From

Cliff Lack joined the Ferodo Band in January of 1954, and eventually found himself sat in the 'end chair' – not bad for someone who thought that if he actually managed to get into the band after his audition it would probably be as a back-row cornet player.

'However, I was finding it difficult, so much so that I told the band's conductor, George Hespe, that I intended to leave. George asked me if I would stay and move down a seat to be assistant principal to Willie Lang. I could not believe what I was hearing – Willie was one of my all-time musical heroes, and I would gladly have paid to sit next to him!'

Cliff Lack of Buxton, 8 September 2008

After the 1955 win at the British Open, Ferodo Works Band was on the crest of a wave, and nothing seemed too much for them: regular concerts, good results at contests and almost weekly broadcasts on the radio, including a visit to London to be part of the popular radio programme What's My Line? *Pictured here along with members of the band are Harry Mortimer, Lady Isobel Barnett, Barbara Kelly, and Nigel Patrick. Willie Lang can be seen standing behing Nigel Patrick.*

there he went to the Ferodo Works Band, under George Hespe, who Willie considered to be a gifted musician. Here was another man who could give a band confidence on a contest stage. Willie often told of the occasion George was rehearsing the heavy section of the band and they were really 'turning out some weight' when suddenly he shouted at one of the bass players as they played a descending passage in unison. One could see the puzzled looks on the players' faces: how could he could pick out one wrong note and also name the player? When they came to the end of the passage, George Hespe said, 'I couldn't hear you, but I could see your fingers ...'

Whilst at Ferodo, Willie was asked by Sir John Barbirolli to join the Halle Orchestra as third trumpet and first cornet. His last appearance with the Halle was in November 1960 after which he moved to the London Symphony Orchestra as their new principal trumpet. In 1988, after twenty-seven years of distinguished service with the LSO, he retired and with his wife Anne returned north and made their home in Harrogate. He died in December 2006.

During his years with the London Symphony Orchestra he worked with composer John Williams on the soundtracks to the *Star Wars* and *Superman* films. He was also one of the trumpet players who played William Walton's music for the film *The Battle of Britain* and other films such as *The Guns of Navarone* and *Where Eagles Dare*. He also worked with musician Frank Zappa and Mike Batt of The Wombles fame. After Willie left Black Dyke in 1953 and went to Brighouse and Rastrick Alex Mortimer was heard to say 'Yes, Black Dyke can still play and carry on without Willie Lang, but it can play a lot better with him.'

ST HILDA'S COLLIERY BAND

South Shields can proudly boast of one of the most famous and successful brass bands in the early history of the brass band movement, the St Hilda's Colliery Band. This band was formed in 1869 when a group of workers, who were mainly from a local coal mine, approached John Dennison, a brass band enthusiast who worked at the local Jarrow Chemical Works, to help them form a brass band. Interestingly none of those asking could actually play a brass instrument and it is recorded that the inaugural rehearsal the principal cornet player was the conductor's ten-year-old son Robert (Bob) Dennison.

The band performed at its first contest in 1874 at Windy Nook, near Felling. This event was a march competition and each of the ten participating bands had to play two marches of their own choice. At the end of the competition the adjudicator, William Lax, made his deliberations and the winners were awarded their prizes, but there was no mention of the St Hilda's band. However, the determination of the St Hilda's players and management was such that they issued a private challenge to the winning band, appointing an adjudicator and referee at their own expense. They proved themselves the worthy winners.

In 1906 the band was known as the South Shields Borough Band, but reverted to its original name with its adoption by the St Hilda's Colliery Miner's Lodge, of the Durham Miners' Association. In the same year Mr John A. Greenwood became the band's professional conductor, and five years later Mr James Oliver was appointed bandmaster, having attained success in the North East with a number of other bands in the area, notably the Heworth and Felling Colliery Bands. He had been a playing member of the band from 1910.

It was partly due to the hard work of James Oliver and James Southern, the band's secretary and trombone player, that the band achieved such rapid progress. In 1912 William Halliwell, the most successful brass band conductor at this time, took over as professional conductor and led them to become the national champions. St Hilda's Colliery Band could be said to have achieved near contest invincibility after winning the 1920 and 1921 Crystal Palace National Brass Band Festival 1,000 Guineas Challenge Trophy. By 1926 it really was regarded as the greatest band of all time. Black Dyke had only its 1902 win behind it and Foden's were not in the races (until St Hilda's was barred from contesting).

By 1926 the band was at the height of its success – it had won five Nationals and had full summer bookings. Its winter appearances in 1928 included Bertram Mills at the Olympia Circus, London. However, with the St Hilda's Colliery having gone on strike in 1925, band members were deemed to be professional musicians and no longer eligible to contest.

In 1927 the band did turn professional, but a number of the players were unwilling to make music their livelihood and decided to leave. However, through the efforts of James Oliver and James Southern a competent band was soon fulfilling its busy

The Eastbourne Redoubt Bandstand and the famous St Hilda's Colliery Band, 1926. It was here that the band performed as part of their two-week annual engagement, playing to thousands of enthusiastic supporters. The band is conducted by James Oliver. On the right is solo trombone player Harold Laycock, and on the extreme left-hand side is soprano cornet player James Dawson. The principal cornet player was possibly Alwyn Teasdale.

concert schedule and from 1928 the band was known as the St Hilda's Professional Band. In 1927 Hubert Bath was appointed the musical director for most of that season, with James Oliver returning the following year and conducting the band until 1933. Following his departure, Australian champion cornet player Frank Wright was appointed for the 1934 season. On his departure to London at the end of that year the band had a number of different conductors. They were, however, unable to regain their former glory, and with the advent of the 'talkies', with rising costs and a fall in the number of engagements, it became difficult for the band to maintain its previous high standards and in 1937 they disbanded. Their final engagement was at the Stanhope Show.

The primary reason for the disbandment was the age and ill-health of James Southern, who had been on the road with the band from 1920. Other important factors (such as the cost of top players and their availability for a long season's employment) made it time to retire. James Oliver bought a house in Brandon near Durham City and continued conducting. James Southern retired to the Wirral. The name of St Hilda's Colliery Band is firmly established in the annals of brass band history – a name which not only recalls a great band, but the halcyon days of an era when our summer seasons were filled with the sound of open-air brass band music.

JAMES SCOTT

'One of life's true gentlemen'

James Scott, pictured above with members of the Cammell Laird Band in 1964, was born in Farnworth, a Lancashire mill town, into a musical family in March 1925. His father, Archie, was employed as a miner, and was also a member of the bass section in the famous Besses o'th' Barn Band. From his childhood days James well remembers walking the eight miles regularly to Besses' bandroom with his dad, where he would sit and listen on a wicker basket (where the band kept their music).

Enoch Jackson was the band's principal cornet player in those days, and on solo euphonium was Bert Sullivan. This was someone James was to get to know very well, as many years later he would be invited to join the Kettering-based Munn and Felton's Band, and Bert was then the band's solo euphonium player. It was whilst watching Enoch Jackson that James said to his dad, 'I want to do that' – not just play like him but be able to commit solos to memory. This he achieved: in his later years he never used music when he stood up to play a solo performance.

It was as a young cornet player with Eccles Borough Band that he heard Munn and Felton's playing their 'lap of honour performance' at the Crystal Palace in 1935. Once again, James said

James Scott with members of the Cammell Laird Band, c. 1964.

James Scott collecting the second prize cheque for 150 guineas at the 1965 National Brass Band Championships presentation on behalf of the Cammell Laid Band. The band was drawn No. 14, to play Gilbert Vinter's Triumphant Rhapsody. *This was James's second time in the championship section National Finals, and was just the start of many prizes he would be awarded as a winning conductor.*

to his dad, 'I want to play in that band.' Little did either he or his dad know, but within twelve years he would be the cornet soloist at the Munn and Felton's Band.

Moreton Secondary School Band after winning the Crosby Music Festival in 1968. James Scott was the conductor. Former cornet player with this band, Stephen Cooke, remembers the music they played to win: Puppet on a String *and* The Golden Cockerel *– happy days!*

The first local concert he attended was with his dad, and that was to hear the Wingates Temperance Band at a local cinema following their success at becoming the 1931 Crystal Palace champions. Another lasting memory was being taken to hear the mighty Foden's Motor Works Band, at Bolton Town Hall. On that day he heard them play *Seven Suite*, which had been written by Edward Elgar for the 1930 Crystal Palace Championships. It was Foden's, under its conductor Fred Mortimer, that were crowned champions that year. Another treat for young James at that performance was hearing Harry Mortimer play *Alpine Echoes*, and all this before he had even started at school.

He was given his first cornet on his eighth birthday and had his first cornet lesson with Herbert Brookes, a local man, and a well-respected cornet player. James made rapid progress under Herbert's tuition, so much so that he was then given lessons by Clifton Jones, the famous Irwell Springs principal cornet player, and in his later years the same position with the Bickershaw Colliery Band.

At the age of nine James was taken to join his first band, the Ellenbrook and Boothstown Band, and can recall going out with the band carolling during the Christmas of 1933. At the ripe old age of ten, James was on the move, joining the Eccles Borough Band as its new third cornet player. This was also the band his father had joined after he had left Besses'. On Monday, 2 September 1935, James stepped out on to the stage at the Kings Hall, Belle Vue, to take part in his first September contest (which was to later become known as the British Open Championships) as the youngest member of Eccles Borough. He was also the youngest player on Saturday, 28 September 1935, when he played at the Crystal Palace, taking part in his first National Brass Band Championships.

At the age of fifteen he was invited to be the principal cornet player with the City of Coventry Band, under the baton of George Thompson, and recalls playing at the band's first radio broadcast. In 1942 George Thompson left to join Grimethorpe Colliery Band. In June of that year George approached James's father and asked him if he would bring him along to one of their rehearsals. After the rehearsal, and still only eighteen, James was appointed the principal cornet, at what was then one of the brass band movement's rising stars.

His move to Munn and Felton's Band in 1947 developed him from being simply a good player into one of the foremost cornet players of his generation. As the principal cornet he became Champion Cornet of Great Britain in 1959 and 1960.

Youngsters often complain these days about having to wear a uniform, but back in the early days at Munn and Felton's the uniform James had to wear was similar to the uniform of the Dragoon Guards: a tight jacket with the Austrian style knots across the front, the kind of jacket the lion tamer at Belle Vue would have been more at home wearing. A shiny leather belt with a shiny black pouch was fastened on the back – and there had to be no finger marks on the shiny leather either. The tight trousers had the traditional wide red tape running down the outside of each leg, and the elasticated strap that went under each of the black shiny boots, and to finish it off you had to wear a cape which had a red silk type of material lining as well.

James conducted the Rochdale Band in 1972 at the Royal Albert Hall, standing in for the band's regular MD Norman Ashcroft, who that day was competing against us as a member of the cornet rank of the Fairey Band. The test piece was *A Kensington Concerto* by Eric Ball and opens with the solo cornet unaccompanied for about eight bars – talk about a baptism of fire for a young twenty-two-year-old lad making his first appearance at this awesome venue!

'We drew number six and the hall was packed because Black Dyke [who went on to win the contest] were on after us and obviously the crowd wanted to get settled before they came on!

The adjudicator's bell sounded and within five seconds there was a deadly hush but for the odd cough from around the audience. James looked at me to start the piece and I discovered that my mouthpiece was somewhere in the middle of my left cheek trying to find my embouchure!

The real pro that he was (and still is), he put down the baton and said encouragingly "No rush David, when you're ready!"

Some seconds later, which felt like half an hour, I managed to find what vaguely resembled my normal mouthpiece position and gave James the nod. Away we went, and I'm pleased to say that I played a good show, but wow what an experience!'

David Morris – principal cornet at the Rochdale Band, 1970-80

By 1948, however, the days of the heavy uniform were finally numbered. The band was issued with a new – and more importantly, much lighter – Mess type uniform. James recalls that Foden's Motor Works Band was the first band to use that style of uniform. This was timed for their 1936 South African tour and participation at the Empire Exhibition in Johannesburg.

For every job they were issued with very strict instructions on times, venue and which of their eventual four uniforms they would have to take with them. James also recalls the gruelling concert schedule. In a three-week season of concerts in Scarborough, for example, the band used to do three concerts every day with just a Saturday evening off.

On one occasion the band was playing under the protective cover of a marquee in Plymouth, and the weather outside was almost at gale-force conditions. It became so bad that it almost blew the marquee away. Once the concert was finished, the band members made the dash for the coach and onto their next concert, which was in Scarborough. In the comparative comfort of the coach, James and the lads were looking forward to getting a few hours of sleep. This hope was short-lived, however, as, whilst travelling down a steep hill in Exeter, the brakes failed on the coach. The driver was forced to steer into the grass banking at the side of the road in order to bring the coach to a standstill.

Just what Bertie Felton thought about it as he followed the coach in his Rolls-Royce has never been recorded, but he made the dash to Exeter to try and organise a replacement coach. Having failed, he even tried to secure the services of an aeroplane to take the band! In the end the band missed the afternoon concert in Scarborough, which in the eyes of Bertie was a disaster. Mind you, James heard later that the marquee the band had played in at Exeter had been blown into the sea ...

The spring of 1960 saw the arrival of a letter from the managing director of Cammell Laird's shipyards at Birkenhead, asking him if he would be interested in becoming the musical director of their works' band. This took a great deal of serious thought. However, he decided to take the plunge and conduct a band.

He moved back North and began what was to become a successful conducting career. At the same time he was gaining valuable experience as a trumpet player with the major northern symphony orchestras. These included the Liverpool Philharmonic, City of Birmingham Symphony Orchestra and the BBC Northern Symphony Orchestra (now the BBC Philharmonic Orchestra).

James Scott with Brighouse and Rastrick, winners of the 1973 National Finals.

James led the band to its first appearance in the National Finals at the Royal Albert Hall in 1964. The pinnacle for James with the Cammell Laird's Band was the following year, when the band took the runners-up prize behind the champions, Fairey Aviation Works Band.

During his career he has conducted many of the best British brass bands, including: Brighouse and Rastrick, Grimethorpe Colliery Band, Foden's, Wingates, Whitburn, Tredegar, and Yorkshire Imperial Metals Band. In 1994 he took Northrop Silver to become first section champions.

Following the departure of Professor Walter Hargreaves after the 1972 National Finals, the search was on to find a replacement at Brighouse and Rastrick. In early 1973 an approach was made to James, which he accepted. His arrival made an impact immediately, when he led the band to first place at the Royal Albert Hall.

In 1975, following Brighouse and Rastrick's success at becoming the Granada Band of the Year, he left to take a similar position at Foden's Motor Works Band. His Midas touch soon followed, and Foden's were crowned Champion Brass Winners at BBC TV North West. Similar success, however, did not follow the next year or in 1977 at the Nationals.

In 1977 James was awarded the 'Iles Medal' by the Worshipful Company of Musicians of the City of London. In 1984, alongside William Relton and Sir David Willcocks, he was invited to adjudicate at the National Finals at the Royal Albert Hall. The following year he was back at the Royal Albert Hall, only this time he was conducting Yorkshire Imperial Metals Band and guided them to a very creditable third place.

During the early 1990s the concept of a band comprising of the more experienced members of the brass band world was being discussed by some of these veteran players in the dark corners of local hostelries. The first thirty names were easy, and the result was the birth of the 'Kings of Brass'. Choosing who should conduct such a musical team was probably the easiest task of all: James Scott and Geoffrey Whitham. James was associated with Kings of Brass until its final concert in the Isle of Man in May 2001. This was not the first time that James had been involved with a band of this kind as during the late 1960s and early 1970s he was involved with the 'Virtuosi Band of Great Britain'.

While James now spends much of his time adjudicating and conducting at band contests and music festivals, both at home and abroad, his services are still in demand at the highest level.

I first met Jim Scott when I was in my early teens (around 1965). He was appointed brass tutor for Wirral schools and I was fortunate enough to have weekly lessons from him. He was a terrific tutor, with bags of experience and ability plus a seemingly endless knowledge of the subject.

I also played under him at Cammell Lairds for a couple of years. I believe he then spent some time with Brighouse before coming to Foden's. He invited me to come to Foden's in 1976 where he had been given the task of rebuilding the band. The band had been together for quite a long time and played to a very high standard, but some new blood was required. He was very keen to instil pride in the players and to bring the name Foden back to the very top of the banding movement ... I can remember that only the highest quality playing would be accepted and the band was worked very hard to try and achieve this ...

Steve Cooke, who had connections with Foden's Band for over twenty-five years

JAMES SHEPHERD

'The famous Newbiggin-by-the-Sea cornet player'

When I was fifteen, I received a letter written on pale blue writing paper. The letter was an invitation to play in a band, and not just any old band: the letter was signed by James Shepherd. No, it can't be – an invite to play in Black Dyke? Of course it wasn't; that was just wishful thinking! James had a Saturday morning school band in Elland in the 1960s, and it was an invitation to play in this band. I have never forgotten the day I received that letter, and I still have it.

James Shepherd is without doubt one of the finest players of his generation. He was the man who led the Black Dyke Mills Band, under the baton of resident conductor Roy Newsome and professional conductor Geoffrey Brand, through one of its most successful periods in the 1960s and very early '70s.

He took those first tentative steps on to the stage at the Newbiggin Salvation Army Citadel, and performed that well-loved standard for all beginners, *Bless This House*. It is hard to imagine him ever being nervous before a performance, but it is said that before performing he went to pray. Someone was obviously listening that day, because he walked out, performed like an old trooper and won the competition.

His first private tutor after his father was Billy Lidster, the euphonium player at the North Seaton Band. It wasn't long after these early performances that James began to be noticed. Beginning as 'a learner', just as we all did, he was introduced to George Wright. George was to be one of his early tutors, and conductor of the Newbiggin (senior) Band at that time, someone James still has the highest regard for.

In one of his later performances, he and the Versatile Brass were asked to perform at the Berlin Philharmonic Hall in front of a capacity audience. It was to be broadcast live on German national radio and also on the BBC's *Friday Night is Music Night*. He played a perfect performance of the old favourite

Jim Shepherd during his time in the Royal Army Medical Corps Staff Band.

I have known Jim since 1962 when he came to help Black Dyke on some engagements. [He] was eventually persuaded to join full-time in May 1963 ... This was in the middle of his 'hat-trick' of wins at the prestigious British Solo Championships. Throughout the long number of years I have been involved in the brass band movement I can say that Jim is the most accurate cornetist of all time: his articulation and production of sound is second to none.

Geoffrey Whitham – Black Dyke Mills Band, musical director of Hammond Sauce Works Band, conductor, teacher, adjudicator, and a friend of long standing

Above: *Jim at thirteen, standing between two family friends.*

Below: *Father and son at Ashington Methodist church, 1960.*

Pandora, said to have been one of his finest solo performances. In 1954, his time had come to do his National Service. His two years were spent in the Royal Army Medical Corps Staff Band at Aldershot under the direction of Lt-Col Louis Brown MD.

He stayed on in the regulars for another year, concentrating on musical performance. This gave him the opportunity of practising the famous cornet tutor book of Jean Baptiste Arban, day after day throughout his service.

His father had been a miner and was determined that his son would not follow the same path for his future employment. Within three months at Aldershot he was appointed the band's principal solo cornet player, taking over what in band circles is known as a 'red lip player', someone whose lips couldn't last long. This gave James the chance to work at his technique and further develop his potential.

Looking back now, those who have had the opportunity of listening to him playing live or on a recording can appreciate just how those hours of practice have paid off: his articulation and technical brilliance are widely recognised.

On his return home in 1957 his reputation as a cornet player began to spread, and many considered him to be a rising star. This new-found local fame saw him leave the Newbiggin Band, following an invitation to join the Pegswood Band as its principal cornet – a band he still remembers as being very enthusiastic and socially one of the best bands he was to be involved with.

In March 1960 he entered the Northumberland League Solo and Quartet Contest, just one of the many senior solo competitions he was to take part in over the next few years. He played an arrangement of Chopin's *Nocturne*, and was awarded the senior soloist winner's prize, a result that he was to be become quite accustomed to.

He made rapid progress and was eventually 'spotted', and invited to Yorkshire to join Carlton Main and Frickley Colliery Band under the direction of Jack Atherton.

It was whilst Carlton was on its way back from the Edinburgh Festival Invitation Contest that Jack Atherton called unannounced into the Co-op, where James had started working after his National Service, and basically gave

When the Black Dyke Juniors Band was disbanded, the instruments were shared out between three junior schools in the Queensbury area. Here we have head teacher Mr Smith with some of the children at Foxhill First School, one of three schools to benefit from the distribution of instruments between 1967 and 1969. James Shepherd, who was a local peripatetic music teacher for the West Riding County Council as well as the principal cornet at the Black Dyke senior band, shares in the school's delight of the unexpected gift.

him two choices: 'stay in Newbiggin and be a grocer, or come down to Yorkshire and get into the business of banding'. These words were enough to persuade James to go south and join Carlton. He made an early impact on the Yorkshire band scene, and was declared the Champion Soloist of Great Britain for three years running during the 1960s.

The position of principal cornet at Black Dyke Mills Band became vacant following the move by Maurice Murphy to the BBC Northern Symphony Orchestra as the principal trumpet player in the February of 1962. This created a serious problem for Black Dyke Mills: who could they get to step into the shoes of a man who was to become a brass band legend?

In April of 1963 James was invited to be the guest principal cornet at Black Dyke's summer engagement at Cliffe Castle, Keighley. At the conclusion of the concert he was heard to say that he felt the band had such a big sound they were far too strong for him; he doubted whether he was really good enough, not only to join but also to lead this world-famous band. (Sentiments that most of the principal cornet players to perform with Black Dyke have echoed.) However, with a little persuasion, he was eventually convinced that with a little time and patience the band would work with him. It took three months for both James and the band to settle in to each other.

In 1971 James was presented with the Insignia of Honour, an annual award presented to a working instrumentalist who has given long years of devoted service coupled with a singular contribution to brass bands.

He led Black Dyke through one of its most successful periods until he left in 1973 to lead his James Shepherd Versatile Brass ensemble, a band which at that stage very few people had heard of. Many thought this would be a short-lived novelty, but the ensemble went on to perform around the world, and along with many broadcasts, television appearances and recordings, its success far exceeded everyone's expectations. His connection with the group was to last twenty-five years. Both he and the members of the ensemble received enthusiastic reviews wherever they performed, travelling to almost all four corners of the world.

Above: *James Shepherd, the only soloist to win the coveted Champion Soloist of Great Britain award three years in succession. Here he is being congratulated by Jack Atherton.*

Left: *Playing a duet together; James Shepherd and the band's assistant principal cornet player David Pratt, who was a member of Black Dyke Mills Band from 1945-46 and from 1953-70.*

Recalling Jim Shepherd is to be reminded and to 're-hear' a stream of golden cornet tone, which never fails to provoke feelings of sheer pleasure and joy. Quality brings its own special message. My years during the late 1960s and early '70s as professional conductor of Black Dyke Mills Band meant that I enjoyed regular contact with many fine instrumentalists, all of who were dedicated to musical excellence. In the pursuit of a golden sound, none was more 'golden' than Jim.

Whether in the bandroom (I cannot recall Jim ever missing a rehearsal), concerts or contests, his technique and control never faltered. Jim Shepherd is an artist of the cornet, an accolade justified by very few.

As the principal cornetist Jim was featured as a soloist on most Black Dyke Mills Band concerts. His many recordings bear testimony to a remarkable ability. Listen to his triple tonguing – a model of even articulation – his quality of sound over the whole range, his spacing so that the music never sounds hurried or pushed along, his ease of performance so that one forgets the technical feats being encompassed. I could go on, but the recordings – available for all to enjoy – say it all.

Alongside his musical qualities Jim Shepherd exudes a natural modesty. He is always willing to offer his knowledge and experience, courteously, sincerely and generously.

It remains a special satisfaction to have shared years of musical endeavour, which have been enriched by a friendship built on admiration and respect. Thank you, Jim, for it all.

Geoffrey Brand, ARAM, LRAM, ARCM, Professional Conductor Black Dyke Mills Band (1967-1974)

The James Shepherd Versatile Brass. The members of the ensemble did change from the time to time, and this photograph shows the 1976 line-up. Back row, from left to right: J. Graham Walker, David Moore, Gordon Higginbottom, David Horsfield, Stephen Thornton, James Shepherd and Ian Copland. Front row: Colin Aspinall, Harvey Whiteley and Robert Atkinson.

In 1972 James Shepherd invited me to become the first conductor of his newly-formed all-star Versatile Brass. I had met James many years earlier, when we were doing National Service with our respective Royal Army Medical Corps and Royal Army Service Corps Staff Bands. With no repertoire available for such a unique combination, arrangements had to be written for Versatile Brass's inaugural concert, held at Uppermill's Civic Hall. Their first two LP recordings, James Shepherd Versatile Brass and Decca Sounds of Brass Series, Vol. 14. *Mardi Gras, Waltz No. 1, La Legende de la Pusta, Barbie* and *Radetzkiana* were just some of the new arrangements which I scored and introduced to the group. Versatile Brass was unique, as was its leader. James Shepherd was a legend of his generation and a true gentleman. It was an honour to have been invited to become associated with Versatile Brass.'

Dennis Wilby, musician, conductor, adjudicator and the first conductor of the James Shepherd Versatile Brass

James Shepherd Versatile Brass, 1978. From left to right, back row: Derek Southcott and Ian Copland. Middle row: Harvey Whiteley, Gordon Higginbottom, David Moore, Colin Aspinall. Front row: James Shepherd, Stephen Thornton, David Horsfield, Graham Walker.

During his long career he has taught countless individual pupils, with many of them going on to join some of the finest brass bands, orchestras and military-styled bands in the country. While he has taken the odd masterclass, he is in his element when confronted by a group of youngsters who are taking their own first tentative steps, and as yet have little or no ability. James has the patience and rare talent of being able to get the best out of his young students. He is known to be a hard taskmaster, but all his young students think the world of him and endeavour to do their best for him, a rare talent indeed. This 'Pied Piper of Banding', as someone once called him, has also been a successful conductor and band trainer, taking his raw recruits on that difficult but highly successful journey from the Youth Section through to the Championships Section of the contesting world.

Along with all those other 'crinklies', as they were once referred to on a brass band radio programme, James completed seven years with the Kings of Brass. Having seen most of the band's concerts and bought the CDs, it has been a treat to see and hear 'Gentleman Jim' taking his rightful place and playing as one of the true Kings of Brass.

And finally... Almost twenty years ago, I overheard two small girls who had taken part in the under-eleven section at the annual Elland Silver Band Slow Melody Competition whispering to each other just before the results were to be announced. One said to her friend in a very serious tone, 'I bet you won't win if Jim Shepherd were in it.' A legend indeed.

2

WHO SAYS IT'S A MAN'S WORLD?

Gracie Cole, rehearsing with Besses o'th' Barn Band at the Royal Albert Hall for a Massed Bands concert in 1942.

THE PEOPLE'S
BAND

In the 1950s The People Band (Odhams Press Band) was one of the few championship bands to have female members – Cicely Webb and Joy Carter.

Cicely was a member of the solo cornet section and, after taking private lessons from George Thompson, the conductor, she became a student at the Royal Academy of Music where she gained qualifications in cornet and trumpet performance. She was a member of Odhams Press Band for five years and became the assistant principal cornet player. A popular piece she played in those days was one third of the cornet trio *Three Jolly Sailormen*. Of all the happy memories she had with the band, taking part in the Belle Vue contests during the 1950s were some of the highlights.

Joy recalls that the band playing at the People's Dart Final and the Hughie Green television show. On the contesting front, Joy remembers the two appearances at Belle Vue and playing in the 'boxing ring' with the audience all around, which had a different feel about it to the more conventional setting.

When I was a teenage solo cornet player with Grimethorpe, a young female cornet player named Gracie Cole often played with the band – the reason being that she had just won the Alex Owen competition, and of course, her prize entitled her to choose her teacher. She opted for George Thompson, who was MD of the band at that time. Gracie later played trumpet with the wartime Ivy Benson's All Girls Band and the Squadronaires. Later she married the Ted Heath trombone player, Bill Geldard. She was a brilliant player at a time when girl brass players could be counted on the fingers of one hand. Denis Wright composed a solo for Gracie called *La Mantilla*, which I remember her playing on a broadcast with Grimethorpe, with the composer conducting.

James Scott – conductor, band trainer, adjudicator and a former principal cornet player of some of the UK's leading brass bands until he retired from playing in 1960

BETTY ANDERSON

'I first met Harry Mortimer when I was eight years old'

Gradually more female players were invited to join the championship bands, and began making their own distinctive mark and presence felt; however, the same could not be said for ladies taking up the baton. Looking through the record books, very few ladies have conducted the winning band at the very highest level. One of the first occasions was in 1978 when Betty Anderson conducted Ratby Band of Leicestershire to first place at the Grand Shield Contest at Belle Vue, Manchester. Betty can remember that at one of the rehearsals the week before they made their journey to Manchester, she told her band, 'you can win this competition' – and of course they did.

Looking back over the journey she had from being a young horn player to winning the Grand Shield and meeting legendary brass band figure Harry Mortimer at Ratby's bandroom, her life has been filled with many magical musical moments.

Betty was born in Leicester, into a family that was part of the Abraham Orsini Anderson knitwear company, which had been started by Abraham in the front room of his home as a freelance bag knitter. Betty's father Jim worked in the knitwear business, whilst her mother Ada ran the family home. Betty had three brothers; the eldest, Bernard, died when she was nineteen, but by all accounts had been destined to be a fine trombone player. Neither of her two remaining brothers were musically inclined, so it was left to Betty to follow in her father's footsteps as a brass instrumentalist.

Like her father she became a tenor horn player, and it was likely that her two non-musical brothers were proud of the achievements their sister had made, particularly when she came home from solo contests with cups and medals. However, the downside for them was her incessant home practice!

Betty's father Jim was a member of the now defunct Imperial Band, and was considered to be a good horn soloist; her grandfather was also a horn player in the Leicester Highfields Band, and her uncle Charles was a very well-known conductor and adjudicator during the 1930s and '40s.

In 1938 she was one of only four female entrants in the national solo competition. Over the last seventy years Betty has witnessed many changes in what was traditionally a male-dominated genre. She entered solo contests almost every week, and on more that one occasion the remarks from the judge assumed it was a male player. On one particular occasion Harry Heyes, a well-known brass band conductor in the Midlands, (who could not see the player during their performance) remarked 'this boy plays like a man', so unusual was it for a girl to be taking part.

Above: *This image of Betty with the Ratby Band was the first photograph of a female brass band conductor taken by* The Times, *1970s. (Courtesy of* The Times*)*

Left: *Betty, aged twelve, playing alongside her father, Jim Anderson.*

Having won the Grand Shield in 1978, Betty asked her old friend Harry Mortimer if he would come along to the bandroom so this special photograph could be taken.

The first solo competition she entered was barely five weeks after she had started to play. She was placed fourth in the under-sixteen class, playing *Sweet and Low*, and came away with the prize of 2s 6d.

At the age of eight she met the legendary Harry Mortimer for the first time; her father knew him when they met on the slow melody and solo contests circuits, and 'HM', became a good friend of the family. He was to become Betty's greatest musical hero, and she says to this day that every time she heard him she learnt something new.

In 1944 she made her first broadcast in a programme that was devised by Harry Mortimer, for younger musicians. She also went on to play solo performances accompanied by bands such as Black Dyke Mills and Foden's.

At twelve she decided that conducting was something that she wanted to do even more than play. At the age of fourteen, her father, who was the conductor at the local ATC Band, found that with so few young lads in the band – all of whom wanted to play the melody – there was no one available to play the bass, so Jim took it on and handed his baton over to Betty. She then conducted the band for the remainder of the rehearsal.

As the early years of conducting slipped by, she began to miss playing, and took the opportunity of joining an up-and-coming band at the time, the Leicestershire-based Kibworth Band, which in those days was conducted by William (Bill) Scholes.

It was as a member of this band that she first met Professor Walter B. Hargreaves, who came to help prepare the band for the big contests. Betty recalls that his rehearsals were good lessons on how to actually rehearse a band. The first thing he did was to sling the players to all four corners of the bandroom, with suitable comments about their ability(!); the band would then have a break before he would bring all the players back together again. Betty often wondered if they would bother to come back at all having been told they were rubbish, but come back they did, and enjoyed every minute of it. The contest results the band achieved with his help and Bill Scholes' leadership were quite staggering: straight into the top section, five successful area results and qualification into five National Championship Finals in succession (1965 through to 1969). The first one was just two years after the band had played in the third section. Betty stayed with the band for ten years and then moved to Ratby Band as their new conductor.

Betty was still working at the family business, often seven days a week. At the age of fifty Betty took a very big gamble: she retired from her job so that she could give much more time to her music and take on work as a private tutor. She remembers these years as being some of the happiest and busiest years of her life in brass bands. It was a time when the number of youth bands was on the increase, and as a never-ending number of parents wanted their children to join a band, work for Betty was plentiful.

As the conductor of Ratby Band, a band that was in the ascendancy, she began to attract a lot of publicity for being one of the few female conductors of a brass band. One of the assets Betty seemed to have over some of her male counterparts was she got more involved in helping to resolve personal problems which were affecting her players, some of which would be having a deleterious effect on the player's performance. Betty has always considered that this was part of her duties as a conductor.

Did she ever experience any problems as a woman in a male-dominated musical genre? No, she is very quick to answer. It never occurred to her there would be any problems; she never expected any special treatment, and certainly never got any. In the early days, of course, when she was the only female player in the band, having her father as the conductor did help. However, there was perhaps just the one occasion when she did receive some special treatment during her years at Kibworth Band. When she joined there was a rota for tidying up the bandroom after the rehearsals, but for some reason she was never asked to be part of the rota, and decided not to ask why. There was also one incident worthy of a mention, only because it would simply not happen these days. It was when she was first appointed the conductor of the Imperial Band. The band was playing in the bandstand in the grounds of the De Montfort Hall in Leicester and one her brothers was in the audience. He overheard a lady sitting behind him say to her friend, 'Have you noticed – there's a girl conducting the band!'

'Yes,' said her friend, 'I have been watching her, and she seems to know just as much about the music as the players do', Betty has always considered that remark as very encouraging.

By the early 1970s, Betty Anderson was musical director at Ratby Band and the goal was strengthening the band and reaching the Championship Section. The band won, amongst other competitions, the prestigious W & H O Wills Contest at Kensington Town Hall. In 1973 the Junior Band (now the Youth Band) was formed, under the baton of Betty.

In 1978 the Ratby Band won the Spring Belle Vue Grand Shield competition, enabling it to compete against the best bands in the country at the famous British Open Championships. At this time Betty had the distinction of being the first female conductor ever to take the stage. The meteoric rise of the band under Betty's direction saw it promoted from the fourth section through to the championship section within eleven years. In 1982 she retired from conducting on a full-time basis and went onto enjoy her role in youth work, particularly as chairman of the National Youth Brass Band from 1974 to 1994.

Looking back over her career, and thinking about all the friends she has made over a lifetime in brass bands, the wonderful experiences that she has had and still has in the world of brass bands, the achievement that stands out above all is conducting on Saturday, 9 September 1978, at the Kings Hall at Belle Vue, Manchester, in the British Open Championships. She recalls looking at her back row cornet line, just as she was about to bring the baton down on that year's test piece *Benvenuto Cellini*, and suddenly realising that they were all from the Junior Band, which she had started in 1973. Not one of them was yet fourteen years old; very few in the rest of the band were over the age of seventeen. Moving up from being a struggling fourth section band to perform and take part in this company at the Kings Hall, the Mecca of brass banding, was a tremendous feat which she is very proud to have been a part of.

In 2002 she was once again at the British Open Championship, this time at the Symphony Hall in Birmingham, where she was presented by the Worshipful Company of Musicians with the Mortimer Medal, and again by the Master of the Worshipful Company at their meeting held in London.

Betty Anderson led the way to what brass bands are today; she joined as one of only a handful of female players (and even less than that who took up the baton). Many others have since followed in her footsteps, and perhaps Betty will yet see the day when a woman conducts the winning band at the British Open or the National Championship final.

We were delighted and honoured when the legendary Betty Anderson accepted our invitation to conduct 'Boobs & Brass' at their 2007 annual concert. The programme consisted of light, popular pieces including *The Pink Panther*. Betty put us through our paces but she was not too sure about our 'real live panther'. After a little persuasion, we convinced her it 'would be alright on the night' and it was! This 'anonymous' trombone player emerged from the shadows, attired in a very pink outfit and crept up to join Betty. After a few wiggles and even a cuddle for Betty, I think she lost her heart to him just a little. The girls gave this wonderful lady their avid attention and the respect that she deserves and we were very proud to make her our newest 'Boobie'. She led us through an evening of great music making, and we hope that her first experience of conducting an all-female band did not disappoint.

A lasting memory from all the girls at Boobs & Brass, Northampton's first all female brass band

LYNDA NICHOLSON

'An audition which was electrifyingly good'

In July 2008 the members of the St Helen's Youth Band, along with many of the band's past members, officials and friends, held a lunch party for a special guest. Although it was a sad occasion, it was also a celebration for all the hard work and success their retiring conductor, Lynda Nicholson, had done for the band. Lynda is one of those rare females in the world of brass bands who has played a leading position in some of the best brass bands in the country. She achieved and produced a quality of playing that has seen her in the coveted 'end chair' principal cornet position. This was at two of the finest brass bands, Desford Colliery and Wingates.

Lynda was born in Dulwich in 1957, the oldest of three children; her sister Brenda is a tenor horn player and a former solo horn player at Desford Colliery Band. Her father Reginald was an army musician and played the trombone with the East Surrey Regiment. Once he completed his military service he joined the Croydon Band as its bass trombone player, and it was here that Lynda was first introduced to playing a brass instrument.

As a youngster she attended Wallington High School for Girls in Surrey, and the Royal College of Music Junior Department on Saturdays. As a young cornet player in the 1960s her musical heroes were Derek Garside and James Shepherd. But in 1974 she saw Maurice Murphy live at the Royal Albert Hall playing Ernest Tomlinson's *Cornet Concerto*, and immediately fell in love with the wonderful sound he produced.

Lynda's first tutor was her father, who was then followed by Alf Jarvis (who not only conducted the Croydon Band but was also a tutor at the National Youth Brass Band of Great Britain). She later successfully auditioned to join the National Youth Brass Band in 1969, and not long afterwards she was appointed the principal cornet, a position she held on six courses.

Attending concerts and band events was something she did from a very early age, supporting her father when he was at concerts or a contest. The earliest concert she can recall which made a lasting impact was on a family outing to the Embankment Gardens in London, to a concert given by the CWS (Manchester) Band. The park was so full with spectators you could barely see the band.

Visiting the Royal Albert Hall on contest day was something special and afterwards she was able to visit the players in the dressing room area and collect their autographs. The fact they were all men never occurred to her, nor did she ever imagine that she would one day play on that same stage anytime in the future, but always hoped she would.

She started playing at the age of eight, but her tuition became more serious when she went to the Royal College of Music four years later. Tuition on the trumpet came from Edgar Riches at the RCM Junior Department, with piano lessons, aural and theory lessons as well as concerts with the orchestra. From this early age Lynda's life was her music, with very little time for other interests or hobbies.

She continued to be a member at Croydon Band until she was fourteen, when her father was invited to conduct the Oxted Band in Surrey. She was beginning to be noticed by the more experienced bands in the district. In 1979 she moved to North London following her appointment to the Music Department at Brent Local Education Authority, teaching children, a role that would bring both her and her students great success. She was also appointed as the third solo cornet at the John Laing Hendon Band, under the baton of Don Morrison.

From Hendon she was appointed the principal cornet at Hanwell Band. To many this would have been success in itself, but Lynda was determined to go on to greater things. In 1986 her big break came when Howard Snell, the former principal trumpet at the London Symphony Orchestra and the professional conductor of Foden's Band, appointed Lynda to the position of assistant principal cornet to John Hudson. Lynda recalls her audition with Howard before the band members arrived, and sitting in for the rehearsal, which was very exciting as the players were all so good.

Lynda's first rehearsal following her appointment was also memorable for her. It was early January 1986 and in blizzard conditions. She managed to drive up from London but only as far as Stoke before she had to turn back. Looking back to that day, she believes she was lucky to have got that far, but she's always been very committed!

In 1990 Lynda was on the move again, this time to be the principal cornet at Wingates Band under the direction of David James, who looked after her as she was the only woman in the band at that time. After David left she also left the band, and within no time she was appointed to the principal cornet position at Desford Colliery, which meant working with James Watson, someone she has the highest regard for. Lynda feels that working with James, who was very supportive toward her and the other women in the band, was the happiest time in her whole banding career.

Was there any added pressure being a female player on the 'end chair'? 'Looking back, I did feel an added pressure as a player. I only ever wanted to be respected as a good player, but I did feel I had to be consistently better than anybody else in order to achieve this, which certainly adds to the pressure, particularly on contest days!'

In 1993 Lynda was invited back to Wingates as the principal cornet, but on this second appointment at the band there were so many women in the band that it could have been in serious difficulties without them.

In 1999 Lynda was invited to play for a few months with the Black Dyke Band, but the distinction of being the first female to be registered with Black Dyke falls to tenor horn player Leslie Howie, in February 1999. Since those days the band has seen a number of fine female musicians invited to join the band. Some readers will be able to remember the days when Black Dyke band members' wives were not even allowed to travel on the band bus: thankfully the world of brass bands has moved on a lot since those days. After leaving Black Dyke Lynda decided to retire from full-time playing and concentrate on her conducting, and on teaching. Her association with the St Helens Youth Band has lasted over twenty years, both through the local authority and as a self-employed brass tutor.

Lynda is married to Ian Smith, a professional French Horn player with the Scottish Opera Orchestra, who has a different perspective and musical outlook to that of the brass band. This has widened Lynda's own musical horizons in respect of repertoire, conductors, performers and musical interpretation.

From those childhood musical heroes, additions to the list now include: Howard Snell, David James, James Watson, Edward Gregson, Placido Domingo, Maxim Vengerov and the legendary Maurice Murphy.

Above: *In 1988, Lynda was a member of the famous Britannia Building Society Band, the sponsorship name at that time for the Foden's Band. Those pictured here include John Hudson, Ian Dickman, Lynda Nicholson, Gillian Hinckley, Alan Hose, Christine Withington, Marty Booth, Mark Vause, Stephen Cooke, Paul Cafferkey, Kirsten Thomas, George Thackray, Gary Russell, Rachel Goddard, David Brunsden, James Charles, Nicholas Hudson, Chris Peeling, Mark Bates, Stephen Singleton, John French, Andrew Grady, Ian Mould, Jef Sparkes, Syd Wood, Mark Oldham, Andrea Richards and Jonathan Savage.*

Right: *London and Southern Counties Region third section champions of 1977. Lynda is second from the right in the front row; her father, Reginald, holding the shield, was the conductor.*

Charley Brighton, the celebrated euphonium and tuba player, recalls the great days when he played at Hanwell Band with Lynda. Ian Johnson was the band's conductor.

We had Lynda backed up by Elaine Wolff [Elaine was BBC Young Musician of the Year in 1980 and is now Mrs Elaine Williams, the principal cornet at KM Medway Band, Kent]. These two cornet players were the envy of most bands in the area at that time. Lynda was solid as a rock, of course, and her style very much suited the band at that time. We used to meet regularly at solo contests in our younger days and play all over London ... Lynda was not just a very good cornet player, but was a great person to know as well.

Charley Brighton – principal euphonium at Hanwell Band and professional soloist

Throughout her career Lynda has won many plaudits and prizes, she has made many recordings on CDs, vinyls and live radio broadcasts – and no other cornet player in a top-section brass band can say they have not one, but two Blue Peter badges! (One of them with her sister Brenda, and then a second with the St Helens Youth Band when it won the National Youth Championships.)

A sign of recognition came in 1992 when she was invited by Dr Roy Newsome to become a cornet tutor at the National Youth Brass Band of Great Britain. Then when the National Children's Brass Band of Great Britain was being set up, Lynda was asked to oversee the inaugural course.

These days, Lynda plays with Kirkintilloch Band, and has started a youth band within the Kirkintilloch band's organisation. This new junior band already has thirty beginners who are all very enthusiastic. With Lynda's fine reputation and infectious enthusiasm, you can be sure this band will do well in all their endeavours.

I certainly remember Lynda's audition, which was electrifyingly good ... it started perfectly, a very bold high C, and went on from there. I believe it was a Herbert Clarke solo. There was no wondering about her or sizing up her standards involved, just enjoyment; in any marking scheme of mine she gets 100 per cent. She is the kind of musician I really love, always ready, prepared and inspired. Appointing a woman to such a prestigious position in the band did not come into it, I wanted the best players and Lynda, along with the Withington twins, and Kirsten Thomas, was the best.

She moved on to conducting, so naturally I saw less of her, with the exception of some contact with her at the St Helens Youth Band, where not only was she terrific with the musical side of the band, but she also built up an exemplary organisation. She also did some very valuable work at the Royal Northern College of Music.

Howard Snell, musical director of Foden's Band, 1981-1996

I first met Lynda in 1983 through my family's connection with the Foden Band. Lynda had made the move north from London to play for the band, and was instantly well received into the band's fold. As assistant principal cornet she took over the end chair when the band's resident conductor, John Hudson, took the baton, as he was also our principal cornet player. This was a role that Lynda enjoyed immensely and excelled at.

I was fourteen when I joined Foden's. It was a huge step for me, so the friendship of Lynda was even more important; she would often drive me to concerts and generally keep an eye out for me ... As the years went by Lynda and her husband Ian remained very good friends with my family, and when my first son was born I often visited their house with him for a good old chat and coffee around the kitchen table, reminiscing about the old days.

Over many years of friendship Lynda has always shone as a professional person, and I am sure this has given the young people involved with the many youth bands which she has been connected with, a great motivation to succeed in music generally.

As a person who shows professionalism at every opportunity, Lynda has given so much to music teaching over the years, and I feel very fortunate to have been the friend of someone who has inspired so many.

Jef Sparkes, Eb bass Foden's Band 1984-1988, currently the musical director of United Co-op Crewe and associate conductor at the Fairey Band

SYLVIA RISBY

'Sylvia is a lady who has brass bands in her blood'

Sylvia Risby is not only a respected member of the Middleton Band, but is also held in high regard throughout the Greater Manchester band scene. She can claim not only to have played, but also sung to a crowd of proportions that few in the world of brass bands can match. She has rubbed shoulders with many of the football greats at both Old Trafford and the City ground at Maine Road.

Sylvia was born in 1940 in the small town of Wistaston on the outskirts of Crewe, the only child of Len and Ada Farmer. With the outbreak of war the family moved to the Moss Side area of Manchester, where she attended St Margaret's Junior School and then Chorlton Secondary School. At the age of sixteen she went to the Trades College, where she qualified as a tailoress. However, in later years she had a change of direction, qualifying as a nursery nurse.

This is 1951 and a young Sylvia Risby stands on a wooden box to sing at Old Trafford, accompanied by the Beswick Prize Band. The man holding the microphone is Joe Miles, the band's secretary, who, a few years later, made a new life in Australia. The band's conductor was Albert Risby, Sylvia's future father-in-law and the man who taught her to play the cornet.

Moston & Beswick Band. From left to right, back row: S. Roberts, -?-, R. Edwards, S. Franklin, A. Oldfield, J. Power; S. Farrington, -?-, J. Farrington, C. Slaley, E. Cosgrove and B. Risby. Middle row: R. Dootson, M. Grady, J. Murray, F. Youd, A. Risby (conductor), S. Risby, J. Elston, P. Foden and H. Brookes. Front row: -?-, J. Mason, K. Foden, D. Cornthwaite, F. Youd, B. Earnshaw and J. Oliver.

For as long as she can remember music has been part of her life; her mother always said that she started singing when she was two years old. At the age of six, along with many other young girls of that age, she was encouraged to join dance classes.

Sylvia was soon recognised as a promising young singer and was regularly heard at concerts throughout the North West. By the age of nine she had started piano lessons and was soon entertaining members of her family with her new-found musical promise.

One of her first big solo singing performances was at the Free Trades Hall in 1950, at a concert for the Broughton House disabled war veterans. By the time she was a teenager she had also joined the Levenshulme Orchestra.

In 1950, Sylvia's parents were regular visitors to most home games at Manchester United. It was on one of those visits they first saw the Beswick Prize Band, who regularly performed at Old Trafford. Sylvia's dad had a bright idea of Sylvia actually singing at one of the matches with the band accompanying her.

After that match he wrote to the band secretary Joe Miles, who invited her to a rehearsal for an audition. They were so impressed with her performance that she was invited to Old Trafford with the band. In March 1951 she stood on a box and sang to a crowd of over 40,000.

Her dad bought her first cornet for £8 from Renold's in Manchester, and although she gave it a good try, she could make no sound at all, so back in the case it went. At the age of eleven she

---

The Bluebell pub played quite a role in the band's existence, and any player that came for a blow with the band would be invited to join the other members of the band for a drink afterwards. Sylvia and Bob always made a point of chatting with everybody, and coupled with open discussion about band matters, this gave the band a real family feel. I think quite a few of the band members even thought of Sylvia and Bob as part of their own family.

During the several years I was with the band their commitment was second to none. I thought my attendance was good, but you could have counted the number of rehearsals missed by Sylvia and Bob on one hand.

During my time, the band had a real purple patch on the contesting stage, culminating in the band's appearance at the National Finals at Torquay in 2002. After a couple of years I made the very painful decision to leave Moston and Beswick and join another band. It was ironic that the night I was to inform Sylvia and Bob they announced that the band was being wound up, which was a very sad day indeed.

Daren Blake, former soprano cornet player at Moston and Beswick Band

was encouraged to give it another go, and went for some lessons to Albert Risby, the conductor at Beswick Prize Band. With his guidance she took to playing the cornet like a duck to water. At the age of twelve she played at Belle Vue in the 1953 Grand Shield on second cornet, playing R. Maldwyn Price's test piece, *Owain Glyndwr*, with Albert Risby conducting. She went on to marry Albert's son Brian, who was to serve as the band's secretary for forty years.

Gradually Sylvia progressed along the cornet line, including a period on the flugel, until she was appointed the band's end chair cornet player.

The year 1958 is forever etched in the history and folklore of Manchester United. Sylvia also has memories from the aftermath of the Munich Disaster when she was asked to sing and play with Beswick Prize Band at the highly emotive memorial service.

She was also asked by the officials at Old Trafford to sing and play with the band at the first match after the disaster. This match was a way of saying thank you to the German doctors who had looked after the surviving team members in hospital. The band was also invited to play at Sir Bobby Charlton's testimonial match in September 1972.

I well remember back in the early 1960s playing with the Clifton and Lightcliffe Band at the ground of Huddersfield Town.

'Those were great days, marching and playing round the track; dodging the coins that were thrown down from the stand. I'll give the spectators of those days the benefit of the doubt and say they were aiming for the open collecting sheet rather than aiming at us. Not only did we get a free pie and a drink but we could also watch the match free of charge as well. The money in those days was collected for and on behalf of the Huddersfield and District Brass Band Association. As fewer and fewer bands wanted to go out collecting, our band took it on and collected throughout the season. Eventually the old collecting sheet went and was replaced with those old-fashioned collecting tins.

I collected from high up in the stand, sending the tin along the rows of seats, setting it off at one end with each of the spectators putting a few coppers in and then passing it on. The only time the tin went missing was when the match had started and it was placed on an empty seat, but it soon found its way back again.

Chris Helme

Over the Pennines in Manchester at the 'Theatre of Dreams' stadium they even had brass bands playing as warm-up entertainment for the fans at Old Trafford.

Look around any band and you will see young players striving to get on, all hoping one day they will be good enough to touch the stars. Then you have, shall we say, the more mature members of the band, players who always seemed to have been there. These are of course the ones who rarely miss a rehearsal and have been members of the band for more years than most people can remember.

They have all been loyal servants of the band and whilst some may have had a spell away, possibly even reaching the dizzy heights of bands at championship level, many others have chosen to stay.

For many years Sylvia was the only female member of the band, which she enjoyed because everyone looked after her. Two of the members from those early days were Jack Oliver and Ken Foden, and she still takes time to visit and reminisce about the old days with them.

In her early days she was one of the few females in what was viewed by many as being a male domain. She often thought, given the opportunity, she would have liked to have played with an established band from the championship section, such as the Fairey Band. Sylvia had three children and believes that few women would have had the opportunity of fulfilling their musical ambitions in those days, and that it was treated as nothing more than a hobby for them.

Although she missed out playing in the higher echelons of the banding world, she was still invited to be on both the television, radio and was regarded as a local personality.

Looking back on her long musical career, the saddest time was when Beswick closed down in the 1960s. With members moving away, and few owning motor cars in those days, the band could not survive. However, a new lease of life came in the form of a merger in 1965 with Street Fold Methodist Band; the group became known as the Moston and Beswick Band.

Gradually, over a period of time, the new band edged its way up through the sections from the depths of the fourth through to the first, and other bands in the Manchester and North West areas were beginning to take notice.

After twelve years the band's musical director left, and a number of players also left to join other bands. The remaining players struggled to carry on and in January 2006 the band finally decided to call it day, with Moston and Beswick Band joining a growing list of other bands which have also closed down in the Manchester area. Sylvia was a principal cornet for twenty-seven years, following nineteen years as the assistant principal cornet.

As far as Sylvia is concerned, brass band people are the salt of the earth, and there is no other group of people quite like them. If you've had a bad day, you go to band practice, play music for two hours, have a chinwag with your friends and then somehow things just don't seem so bad after all.

Today she is still enjoying her playing as second cornet at Middleton Band. Two years ago the band was asked to play at Old Trafford for a local Derby match, an event which brought her back many happy memories. The band have a good set of players with a good mix of ages.

She has enjoyed every minute of her fifty-five years in the world of brass bands, and hopes that she can continue to contribute for many more years to come. Even today, after all these years, she is still asked,'were you the girl who sang on match days at Old Trafford and Maine Road?'

I first met Sylvia as a friendly opponent: a fine flugel player for Moston and Beswick Band playing against my band in the third section. I next met her as musical director of her band, now in the first section, a number of years later. The band master had left and, as is often the case, players had followed him to his new band. Sylvia was her usual positive self, willing to be the work horse and do what was necessary both within the band as a player and behind the scenes, quietly ensuring that her father's band still served its community at the highest standard it could achieve, as well as maintaining a positive presence on the contesting scene. This meant that Sylvia had to leave the relative comfort of the back row she had only just managed to 'retire' to, and once again became a mainstay of the front bench. As is her way, no complaints were ever heard, other than self chastisement to continue to improve and deliver her very best at all times; even if the glue on a bridge had just loosened before an important passage.

Her many fond memories with the band included non-playing members collecting money by parading around the edge of the pitch holding up a large bed sheet for the football supporters to throw coins into, until it became too dangerous owing to the increased velocity and accuracy of over-zealous fans at later matches aiming at the collectors rather than the sheet.

Sylvia continued her service to the band after I had left, still filling gaps whenever she could not cajole administrative support, and when the band's name sadly became one of Manchester's historical memories, she maintained her spirit and joined Middleton Band, an up-and-coming band, giving her best in her own inimitable style. Sylvia is a lady who has brass bands in her blood, and no doubt you would find it engraved within her body like a stick of rock might from any famous coastal town.

Martin Obermuller, former musical director of Moston and Beswick Band

KIRSTY ABBOTTS

'I am part of a team, and we all pull together'

Having now read about Gracie Cole, Cicely Webb, Joy Carter, Betty Anderson, Sylvia Risby and Lynda Nicholson, you will have gathered that when they first started playing and joined a band the number of female players was far less than it is nowadays, particularly at the higher level of banding.

Over the last fifty years there have been many changes, including more and more women joining top section bands. With many in principal positions, even more in senior administrative roles in both their own bands and on a regional and national level, we also now have a number of all-female bands.

The number of female conductors is also beginning to rise. Who will follow in the footsteps of Betty Anderson and conduct a winning band at a major competition? Betty's childhood experience at a slow melody competition when the judge, whilst tucked away out of sight, commented that 'with this kind of playing this boy will go far', a remark she can still smile about all these years later, seems unlikely to happen today.

Looking through the membership of some of our top-section bands there are now many fine female instrumentalists, including: Michelle Ibbottson, soprano; cornet players Kirsty Abbotts and Morvern Gilchrist; flugel players Helen Williams, Alex Kerwin, Joanne Childs; horn players Lesley Howie and Sheona White; Becky Smith, trombone; Katrina Marzella, baritone, and Simone Rebello, percussion, just to name a few. There are now more female players than ever, and not just in the championship section bands, but throughout the 500 (approx) registered and 500 (approx) unregistered bands.

I recently read of Kirsty, 'everyone knows in the brass band world she is a quality player who never fails to deliver on the contest stage.' Kirsty is the principal cornet player at the Carlton Main Frickley Colliery Band, which is currently tenth in the brass band world rankings (27 March 2009). As the youngest of the ladies I have included in this chapter, let us take a closer look at her musical life, and see how it has developed from her first tentative steps, from being a member of a youth band to being the principal cornet player of such a high-ranking band.

Kirsty was born in Tiddington, Stratford-upon-Avon, the youngest daughter of Dennis and Margaret Abbotts. As a child, Kirsty grew up in Shipston-on-Stour and was educated locally, with music being very much in the family. Her father played the trombone in Shipston Town Band. Her grandfather was also a noted local singer, and her grandma played the piano and organ at the local church. Her sister Keren is also a very good flautist.

In 1989, Shipston Town Band was awarded first place in the third section South Midlands and East Anglia Area Finals and qualified to compete for a second successive year in the National Finals. Kirsty Abbotts proudly holds the winner's cup, with the band's conductor, Richard Nash, holding the winning band's pendant.

At the age of six, Kirsty was encouraged to play the piano, and then at the age of nine she joined her father in the world of brass bands and was given lessons on the cornet. The local Shipston Town bandroom was literally on the doorstep, and one Sunday morning she accompanied her father to her very first rehearsal. During the rehearsal she went into the instrument store and found an old, battered cornet in an old-fashioned triangular case and decided she wanted to learn to play.

Joining Shipston Beginners' Group, she soon progressed and moved up into the junior band, and by the age of twelve she was the principal cornet. She was soon invited to move up into the senior band, and within three years she was the principal of that band as well. In 1988, Shipston Town Band was in the third section and qualified for the National Finals, something it repeated the following year.

In 1989 Kirsty decided that music was to be her chosen career, it was that same year she left Shipston and moved north to begin her studies at Huddersfield University. She was soon invited to join the Sellers College Brass, as a solo cornet player. It was at Huddersfield that she met her musical hero, Philip McCann. Kirsty then had a stint playing flugel, repiano and as assistant principal. In 1995 she was promoted to the 'end chair' by Philip McCann; this came at an important time in her career, and could be said to be one of those defining moments that would have a lasting effect on her future in brass bands.

The promotion came just before the National Championship Yorkshire Area Finals in Bradford; the band, conducted by Philip McCann, were all on top form that day, and awarded second place, which meant qualification for the National Finals in London. The band's visit to

Kirsty Abbotts performing a solo with Sellers International Band.

the Royal Albert Hall soon came around, and under the baton of Frank Renton took a very creditable seventh place.

In 2002 a new opportunity presented itself and Kirsty, although a little sad about leaving after so many years with Sellers, was given the chance of joining Carlton Main Frickley Colliery Band. The invitation came from the band's new musical director, William Rushworth, and was an opportunity not to be missed. She initially agreed to help out for six months. When Kirsty joined, the band was going through a process of re-building and consolidation. Kirsty was on the front-row solo cornet position, and it came as quite a shock to find that she and Kenny Ralfe were the only two front-row cornet players.

The one redeeming feature in those first few rehearsals was that the few players the band had at that time were all determined to work hard and re-establish the name of Carlton Main Frickley Colliery Band. This was also a new experience for Kirsty, to be part of a top-section band with such a long history that meant so much to so many people. After seven years, has it been the right choice? 'I have loved being part of this famous old band, and still do.'

Throughout her playing career at Sellers and during her seven years with Carlton she has felt no added pressure or resistance as a female in a high-profile position, in what is now such a highly rated – indeed top ten – band in the current world rankings (March 2009). 'This may happen elsewhere, but not in these bands. I am part of a team, and we all pull together to ensure the band is on its way back to becoming one of the country's leading brass bands again, where it has been throughout most of its long history.'

Looking back and thinking about the people who have helped her, Philip McCann is very high on her list. 'Whilst we didn't always agree during the years I was at Sellers, I have always had respect for him and appreciation for the tuition he gave me, and the discipline he instilled which is required to achieve and then maintain a standard to retain the seats I have held.'

53

Looking through Kirsty's list of achievements her stature as a principal cornet in one of the country's leading bands is continuing to grow. Her achievements include: British Open Cornet Champion in 2003; Best Principal Cornet at Brass in Concert in 2000/2003 and 2004; Best Soloist at the Mineworkers Contest in 2005; Best Instrumentalist at the Grand Shield in 2006; and 4barsrest Best Instrumentalist at the Scottish Open Brass Band Championships in 2006.

It now seems a long way back to the days of watching Cory Band, which was the first top-section band she was taken to see at a local concert. The principal cornet player, Jim Davies, made quite an impression. In October 2006 she recorded her first CD, accompanied by Carlton Frickley Colliery Band with conductor Allan Ramsey. Of all her achievements, this is one that she is particularly proud of. A recent comment about the CD read 'Kirsty's playing is breathtaking'.

Looking back over the history of the individuals featured in this chapter, Kirsty is certainly one of those leading the way, moving on from the days when female instrumentalists were rare in brass bands, and even more scarce in the championship section bands. To have a female principal cornet player would have been unheard of not long ago.

As a young teenager, following a trip to the home of the Brontës at Haworth in West Yorkshire, Kirsty always wanted to live in Yorkshire, and one day she wanted to be the principal cornet in a Yorkshire band. She has been asked on a number of occasions about how far she wants to go in brass bands; further opportunities have been offered but she enjoys playing with Carlton. She firmly believes that being part of a successful team is more important, and gives her more satisfaction than aiming for higher things for herself. Kirsty's outlook on her musical career is that she loves playing and never wanted it to become something that completely took over her life.

Kirsty has come a long way from her days in Shipston Junior Band. On one of the first occasions she stepped forward to play a solo, the old John Hartmann cornet solo *Weidekhr*, the baton came down in front of a packed concert hall, but for some inexplicable reason the whole band failed to start – except Kirsty, who, endeavouring to be a very young professional, played the whole of the opening theme as a solo. Whilst this was very embarrassing, the applause was rapturous and her father, who was conducting, was very proud of her.

Looking back on her career, there are many memorable moments, but she really feels that the happiest memories involve all the great friends she has made, and of course making her parents proud.

Betty Anderson said that things had to change, and Kirsty and all the other female players, particularly those in the higher echelons of banding, are a testament to that change. Whilst Betty inspired many young female players during her career, today's generation of female players will equally inspire the young players of tomorrow.

There is little doubt that Kirsty Abbotts is one of the finest traditional cornet players in the banding world at present and she has demonstrated that to the full wherever she has performed. The art of true lyrical cornet playing is not dead.

Kirsty is a superb exponent of what is fast becoming a dying art and does it splendidly on the fourteen tracks on show on this enjoyable release. Lovely phrasing, precise production, warmth of tone and a clear understanding of the musical line – it is a joy to listen to. Catch it whilst you can, because the next generation of cornet players in particular are not being taught to play in this way.

Review comments from 4barsrest.com following the release of Kristy's CD, 'Soliloquy'

3

A FAMILY AFFAIR

Fred Muscroft with his wife Judy and daughter Linda.

THE MUSCROFT FAMILY

Fred Muscroft was born in London, but spent his formative years in the Leeds area where he was brought up in a musical household. His father was a solo cornet player in the Life Guards, and a professional musician. Being so busy, he did not have the time to teach young Fred how to play the cornet. However, his grandfather, Oliver, had in his younger days played soprano in the old Armley & Wortley Band in Leeds, and was able to give Fred his early tuition. Fred recalled when his grandfather used to tell him about the day the band played at one of the old Crystal Palace contests. With his grandfather playing 'sop' and his dad playing 'solo cornet' that day, it was inevitable that young Fred would become a brass player as well.

He made good progress, and by 1937 he was the principal cornet of the now defunct Leeds Model Band. It was whilst he was a member of this band that, on 23 June 1935, he broadcast his first solo, playing the well-known cornet solo by Harold Moss, *The Nightingale*, at the age of eleven. He later went to London to study music at the Royal Academy. In 1942 he joined the Scots Guards where he served for twenty-two years, with many of those years as its principal cornet. Whilst Fred was gradually building up his freelance work in London, where he was regularly playing with orchestras and big bands, the music scene began to change. During the early 1960s he became disillusioned, and he and his wife made the decision to move back north, which they both considered to be their real home.

Almost straight away he was contacted by the Yorkshire Imperial Metals Band (Yorkshire Imps) asking him to join them. Fred went on to have many successes and happy years with the band, but even after he retired from top-class banding he continued to play with many other music ensembles into his early eighties. Sadly, Fred passed away in October 2007. Many of the fine tributes that were published by the band press included the words 'One of the true legends of the brass band world'. He wrote many brass arrangements which were often described as 'ahead of their time', and are still regularly played today.

In the 1962 film *The Loneliness of the Long Distance Runner*, written by Allan Shillitoe, the original trumpet theme to the movie was performed by Fred, who was then the principal cornet at the Scots Guards.

The Yorkshire Imperial Metals Band had an impressive cornet line-up in 1976. From left to right, front row: Graham Walker, Fred Muscroft, Raymond Goodall, Graham Etherington. Middle row: Roy Roe, Steve Clayton, Kevan Barlow. Back row: George Spencer, Michael Dylarga, John Muscroft; and creeping in on the right-hand side is Steve Jarvis.

THE FAWBERT FAMILY

Brass banding has traditionally been a family affair. Youngsters joined the learner's group because their dad had been a life-long member, along with other extended family members who were also involved as well. Those of you who joined a band fifty years ago will remember that your mother would not have been left out: she would have been the latest recruit to the all-important ladies' committee. Generally always in the background, they did most of the band's fund raising, and were the band's catering department. They would be the ones who made the pie and peas for the whist drives, the beetle drives, sorted out the orders for the fish and chip suppers, and of course organised the biggest fundraiser of them all, the 'Sale of Work'.

One of those brass band families was the Fawbert family in Derbyshire. I met ten-year-old Andrew Fawbert, who even at that young age was a wonderful euphonium player, at the Workers' Music Association Summer School of Music at Wortley Hall, South Yorkshire, in the 1960s. I soon discovered that he was not the only member of the Fawbert family who could play a brass instrument. I recently read that Marie Smith (*née* Fawbert) was retiring from a lifetime of working with the Shirland Welfare and Training Bands, and was probably the best person to speak to and find out just how many and how long the Fawbert family have been actively involved with brass bands.

Marie was one of four children to Jack and Sarah (always known as Lizzie) Fawbert, and was born in Stonebroom, Derbyshire, where she still lives today. The Fawbert musical dynasty dates back to Marie's grandfather, Thomas, who, having emigrated to America, came back to Pudsey, a small town situated between Bradford and Leeds, with his two children, following the death of his first wife. He remarried, and his new wife was Marie's grandmother.

The long-held story in the Fawbert family is that a rather well-to-do aunt thought that Thomas's children would be bored after moving from Pudsey to rural Derbyshire. Thus a consignment of instruments, including a piano, three cornets, a tenor horn, a trombone and a soprano cornet, were sent from Leeds railway station to Doe Hill station at Stonebroom. This was the first generation of Fawbert's playing brass instruments, in the pre-First World War days as the dark clouds were gathering over Europe.

With this generation growing up in the band world, and then having children of their own, the next generation of Fawbert players were ready to join this family of musicians: cousins Frank, Teddy, Alfie, Philip and Michael, second cousin Keith and then his children Anthony and Rachel. Then along came Marie's brother's children, nephew Andrew and niece Melonie, and of course Marie's own son Nicholas, who as a guitarist is the only non-brass player. As the numbers grew there was almost enough to create their own band. The family on Marie's mother's side included great uncles who played the trombone in circus pit orchestras.

One of her heroes was her Uncle Arthur. Arthur had his own dance band which used to entertain at the Miners' Welfare every Sunday for two hours, and he would often take Marie along. Marie quickly decided that she wanted to learn to play and as soon as a trumpet could be found (and saved up for), it was quickly bought. Off she went to trumpet lessons, learning that dance-band style of playing. As she became more proficient she began doing guest work at clubs and entertain at the local church and WI. Soon Marie was winning many of the slow melody and Air Varie contests.

Every Sunday Marie either played as a member of a quartet for one of her dad's friends, or to piano accompaniment in the family front room. Then it would be a short walk to Uncle Wilf's pub where he would be playing the piano with one hand and the cornet with the other, and all the family would join in. Marie played solos and duets with him. Her Uncle Arthur was not only a brilliant soprano cornet player but also, she recalls, knew all the different soloistic styles required to earn some money from playing, in what were hard times. These included styles of cornet and trumpet players: Raphael Mendez, Kenny Baker, Maurice Murphy, Miles Davis and, in later years, Wynton Marsalis.

It was inevitable as Marie was growing up in the very early post-war years that she would join the rest of the family down at the local Shirland Miners' Welfare Band. In the original bandroom (which was upstairs at the Shirland Miners' Welfare Institute), they had to sit on stools to play – no slouching down in easy chairs. It wasn't long before the band was on the move – just across the road to what was called the Brigade Hall, where there was always a roaring open fire to greet everyone who walked in.

Marie recalls that in her early rehearsals her Uncle Wilf conducted the band, before Mr Brearley took over, but from those early days she particularly remembers Mr Sid Greaves. He was a new conductor who would play the cornet in one hand and conduct the band with the other. Mr Greaves always came to the band rehearsals carrying a small attaché case which seemed only to contain a towel, which he used to mop himself down with after each rehearsal. He seemed to Marie, then still barely a teenager, to be a one-man cornet section, playing almost all the parts.

She was still a young teenager when her father took over as conductor, but soon afterwards she left the band to join the famous Ivy Benson All Girl Dance Band, and toured the world. This was a huge step for a fifteen-year-old girl to take. Marie played with Ivy Benson from 1957 and then went on to play for the Dinah Dee Band, playing in and around Europe. Marie enjoyed the life of a professional musician until the late 1960s.

On the death of her father she left the world of dance bands and went back home. Once back in the family fold Marie joined the Civil Service Benefits Office as her day job, and in the evening she worked in Sheffield as a semi-professional musician. On top of all that she also had brass banding three times a week. It was now that Marie took on the teaching role, which her father had done for so long, beginning with the pupils he had at the time of his death.

This started a twenty-year career with the band. Conducting wasn't the natural musical progression she had anticipated; rather it came about by accident because there was no one else to conduct the junior band or anyone to conduct the quartets. Someone had to do it. As Marie says, 'Better a volunteer than the whole thing coming to an abrupt end, not something dad would have wanted ...'

The Dinah Dee Band performing in Hamburg. Marie is the trumpet player fifth from the right on the front row.

The Shirland Silver Prize Band, seen here in about 1952, really was a family affair. From left to right, back row: Philip Fawbert; Arthur Fawbert; Peter Thompson, champion cornet player Nicholas Thompson's father; Walter Scott, dance band leader; Arthur Fawbert; Mr Needham; Jack Fawbert, Marie's brother. Middle row: Jack Fawbert, father; Reg Tuplin; Douglas Carlin; Douglas College, one of the current band's front room cornet players; Ted Marsden. Front row: Tommy Bunting; Ronnie Thompson; Marie Fawbert, Jack's daughter; Sid Greaves; Lois Williams; Joe Frost; Gladwin Fritchey.

Marie started teaching me in 1976 when I was twelve years of age. She was a great teacher and used to travel up to my home in Sheffield each week to give me a cornet lesson. Marie must have taken me to every slow melody contest north of Leicester in the four years that she taught me, and during that time never charged my parents a single penny. I owe her everything and will never forget what she did for me. Marie taught me how to play musically with good sound and phrasing and also how to sight read. I have never come across another teacher who can teach young children so well – she has that gift. I don't know how she did it in such a short amount of time, but in those four years she transformed me from an enthusiastic little village cornet player into one of the bright stars of my generation ... Marie's commitment to young people is legendary, and anyone who was lucky enough to have that magic wand waved over them went on to success as a player. There are many of her former pupils out there; many have had great careers both in brass bands and as professional players of repute. She is truly a legend and deserves every accolade going ... My mum and dad once told me that they saw her when she was a little girl playing alongside legendary trumpeter Eddie Calvert. They said she was just a little slip of a girl, but boy could she play!

Richard Grantham, assistant head teacher (Hucknall), conductor and composer

Marie ended up conducting both the senior band and junior band, as well as the contesting quartets, but a health problem eventually forced her to resign from the senior band. She continued to conduct the juniors, and this was the start of the Shirland Miners Welfare Training Band, and it went from strength to strength. Although a brass band has existed in Shirland since the 1880s, the Training Band, as it is known, was not formed until 1998. A few parents and their young children who were already learning to play formed the band, and it joined the fourth section where it quickly developed into a tight musical unit. Shirland MW Training went on to win the third section and second section regional titles. As a result of its placing in the 2006 regional championship, the band was promoted into the first section in 2007. It is now known as the Shirland Welfare Band and is in a consolidated position in the second section, with its new conductor Andrew Dennis.

But what has happened to the rest of the Fawbert family of musicians? Marie's brother Jack sadly passed away in 1999, but his contributions to both the local and national brass band scene were immense. He started playing, just as they all did, as soon as he was big enough to hold the instrument, but he excelled in the area of administration, particularly as the Shirland Miners' Welfare Band secretary. Whilst Marie drove the band through to the championship level, Jack was at the centre of the administrative and organisational side of things.

Jack's daughter Melonie, a head teacher now, still finds time to play her cornet for fun, and Andrew, his son, went from Shirland to the Birmingham School of Music. He joined the college band (which through company support later became known as the Jones and Crossland Band). This band had a meteoric rise under the baton of Roy Curran, and for a number of years performed well at the highest level of banding. Andrew went on to be a professional musician and teacher, which included being a member of the Michael Nyman Band. His son Stephen is training to become a percussionist. When time permits is he always available to help out at the band.

Marie's sister Kathleen (always known as Dallas) played tenor horn but after a while she gave up playing. However, her brother Arthur played for both brass bands and local dance bands. Sadly, however, he lost his all-important front teeth owing to an accident at the pit, which ended his playing days. He has been one of the band's most active supporters, selling tickets and programmes at local contests, but at seventy-five has decided that he will retire this year.

Jack's wife didn't play, but like most banding wives she went to every concert and contest, always armed with 'a cart load of snap' (a lot of sandwiches). Tea in a flask was not Lois's way of doing things: she would go with a primus stove, a jug of water and the biggest teapot she had.

Of Marie's uncles Wilf, William and Edward, Uncle Edward was killed in the First World War and his grave is in France. His childhood brass band training came in during his war service, being a bugler boy for the Essex Regiment. Uncle Asa was killed in a mining accident at Glapwell Pit, Derbyshire, and left seven children, with three of the children, Frank, Teddy and Alfie, going on to be brass players. Uncle Arthur, who played for both Shirland Band and Swanwick Colliery Band, even took part in a jazz band contest in Nottingham watched by none other than his musical hero Louis Armstrong. He also made a broadcast from the Crystal Palace which his mother listened to. Sadly, she died the same night – nothing to do with the broadcast, Marie is quick to point out!

Arthur's son, Phillip, was the principal cornet player at Shirland during the 1950s and was a beautiful cornet player. He often turned on the jazz style of playing, just as his father did. Philip's brother Michael followed in the family tradition by taking up the tenor horn, but his heart was not in it. He really wanted to be a percussion player, and after years of regular practice and dedication he would often be seen as the kit player on the local club scene.

In 2007 Marie was presented with the Diploma of Honour of the Worshipful Company of Musicians, in recognition for her contribution to the brass band scene. This was particularly in respect of her work in 'the training and tuition of young musicians', a great honour. Few other families can demonstrate how much brass bands have been part of their lives.

THE OUGHTON FAMILY

To just tell the story of the virtuoso cornet player and conductor Robert Oughton in isolation would be unfair on the rest of what can only be described as a brass band dynasty. So we will begin this story back in the days of his father William Oughton, Snr, a time when Queen Victoria still reigned supreme and the last days of the nineteenth century were drawing to a close. The days when, it was said, there were over 20,000 brass bands throughout the country.

Even in those far-off days music was in the family: William's father Robert was a semi-professional trombonist and played regularly in a pit orchestra at one of Sunderland's largest theatres. As well as being a fine trombone player, he has also been described as a professional gambler – he was seen regularly at the race tracks throughout the North of England, and is reputed to have made a decent living out of his gambling.

Young William was, like many other youngsters in the brass band world, initially taught to play the cornet by his father. The question in the Oughton family was not 'are you going to play?' but 'what are you going to play?' Playing a brass instrument was expected. From the beginning young William showed some promise – so much so, in fact, that he soon outgrew his father as a teacher. Rather than holding him back, Robert found his son another teacher, none other than the legendary Alexander Owen, one of Manchester's sons. His will be a name that few Mancunians beyond the world of brass bands will have heard of, but he was a giant inside that world.

William visited Owen every weekend for two years, and inevitability William's skills as a cornet player developed very quickly. He would travel down from Easington on the Saturday, have a lesson that evening, stay overnight and then have a second lesson on the Sunday morning before returning home on the train. In 1900, at the age of eighteen, he was appointed to Spencer's Steel Works Band in Newcastle. With William in the 'end chair', the band took part in the pre-First World War Crystal Palace National Championships, where it had some moderate success.

Every Thursday evening the owner of the Steel Works Band came to listen to the band, and without fail before he left he always gave William a guinea (which was 21s). William always took the money to the Post Office and bought himself a National Savings Certificate, which at the time of his death in 1961 had increased in value quite significantly. In 1923 he took up conducting at Hetton Band, but after three years he left, having upset the band officials by allowing his son to leave the band and join the famous St Hilda's Colliery Band.

On the 23 December 1927, having seen an advertisement for a new bandmaster at the Dalmellington Band in Ayrshire, Scotland, he applied for the job and was offered the position, which he was very pleased to accept. However, his initial arrival in Dalmellington got off to a bad start: he was due to start work on Christmas Day and Ben Yates, a committee member, was delegated to call on Mr Oughton at 6 a.m. to take him to his new place of work at Dunaskin. He was be met by the retort, 'I'm an Englishman, and I don't work on Christmas Day!'

With the initial falling out resolved, the band gradually began to show some promise, and in 1930 was offered a radio broadcast by the BBC at Radio Scotland. This prestigious event had been arranged by Hubert Bath, who as well as being the well-known brass band composer was also the musical director of St Hilda's, which by this time had become the first and only professional brass band. On the programme was a new solo by Percy Code which he had titled *Zelda*; it was to be performed by William Oughton, Jnr. This created a serious problem because the St Hilda's Band, now being a professional band, was barred from taking part in any of the BBC's brass band radio broadcasts.

William in his Spencer's Steel Works Band uniform. The plumed hat indicated that he was the principal cornet player.

William Oughton Jnr in his St Hilda's Colliery Band uniform in the mid-1920s.

During the early 1930s the band did really well under the baton of William Oughton, but the mid-1930s brought a period of despondency throughout the Doon Valley coalfields. This had a serious impact in Dalmellington as some of the band members who were miners found themselves on short-time working. William himself was down to a two-day working week. Additionally, the band was now unable to pay his remuneration, so he decided it was time to leave. With all three of his sons now making successful musical careers for themselves, he decided to leave Dalmellington and move south. He accepted an offer to become the bandmaster of the Kendal Borough Band, Cumberland, a band that has long since disappeared into the annals of Kendal's local history.

In 1935 William Oughton's second son, Robert, left Dalmellington to join Munn and Felton's Kettering-based band. Cecil, the youngest son, was also a keen musician and played the trumpet, but he turned his back on the world of brass bands and made a successful career in the world of big dance bands instead.

In 1947, having retired from work, William returned to Dalmellington to find his old band struggling in the fourth section. Once again he took hold of the baton and set about dragging them back to those halcyon days of the 1930s. Having managed to take the band to many successful contests by the 1953 contest season, the band was finally promoted back into the championship section. Throughout the 1950s, under William Oughton's direction, the band was regularly heard on BBC Radio in the West of Scotland.

William Oughton, Snr, died on the 1 September 1961 and was interred in Dalmellington cemetery.

WILLIAM OUGHTON, Jnr

William was the eldest son, and as a young cornet player with the Hetton Band in Hetton-le-Hole his solo performances were soon attracting the attention of the best bands in the area. During the early 1920s he joined the legendary St Hilda's Colliery Band as the assistant principal cornet player, sitting alongside the band's famous cornet player Arthur Laycock. When the position of principal cornet became available in 1923, following Arthur's move to the Eastbourne Municipal Orchestra, it was William who was promoted to probably the most famous and prestigious 'end chair' of that time.

St Hilda's won the championships in 1912, 1920, 1921, 1924 and 1926, but were then barred from entering again because its status as amateur musicians came into conflict with the organisers. This conflict came at a difficult time: St Hilda's Colliery had been closed down, the General Strike of 1926 had begun, and the subsequent depression was beginning to bite. With the colliery closed, the band had to choose whether to close or carry on as professionals. James (Jimmy) Southern, their astute band manager, bought all the band's instruments, music library and the charabanc which had conveyed them to their concert and contest venues throughout the country. For the next three years James built upon his vast number of contacts and lucrative concerts the former band had carried out. His daughter Helen was the band secretary and she ran it almost like a travelling orchestra. In 1930, for example, she organised a ten-week tour of Ontario State in Canada, culminating with an engagement at the Canadian Exhibition in Toronto. In 1932 she married William Oughton Jnr. They had four sons, William, Kenneth, Richard and Cecil. Except for Richard, all are now deceased, and none of the children were musically inclined.

By 1937 the dark clouds of war were looming over Europe once again, and the diary of band engagements had all but dried up for St Hilda's. The band performed its last engagement at Stanhope Show, County Durham, on 12 September 1937, which brought an end to a band of some antiquity and pedigree. Once the band had gone, the players themselves either called it a day and retired or moved on, as William Oughton did by joining Farrington's Concert Orchestra playing the trumpet. In 1940 he moved to Newark-on-Trent and joined Ransome and Marles Works Band, as its principal cornet player, which also provided him with employment in what was a reserved occupation. In 1947 James Scott, the band's principal cornet, left Ransome and Marles to join Munn and Felton's Band. The vacant position was given to William Oughton's youngest son Robert, who had just finished his military service.

James first saw William in 1937 when he and his father watched the St Hilda's Professional Band performing in the bandstand at Dover, and recalls he was a very fine player. The first time he actually met him was when he was appointed the principal cornet at Ransome and Marles Works Band in the late 1940s ... James recalls that he had a very strong Scottish accent and was still a very strong and accomplished player. At every opportunity he would reminisce about the old days with St Hilda's, particularly when he sat alongside the legendary Arthur Laycock.
James Scott, who is still in brass banding at the highest level today

---

ROBERT OUGHTON

Robert Oughton was born on the 11 August 1920 in Brandon County Durham, and was the second son of William and Violetta.

Shortly after his eighth birthday he was introduced to the world of brass bands when his father began to teach him the rudiments of cornet playing. By the time he was twelve years old his talents were evident, and as the years went by it was apparent to everyone that he was destined to be a musician.

In 1935 he auditioned and was appointed the assistant principal cornet player to the renowned Elgar Clayton at Munn and Felton's Band, and then in 1937 he was appointed principal cornet player at Grimethorpe Colliery Band. This was in those days a position which was rumoured to be the highest paid 'end chair' cornet player at that time.

It was not long before he was on the move again, this time he went to Blackhall Colliery under the baton of Noel Thorpe, where he stayed from 1938

Ransome and Marles Works Band. In 1951, the band was crowned the British Open Champions after performing The Conquerors *by Eric Ball. The tall man standing in the centre of the back row with no instrument is Robert Oughton.*

to 1941. After his wartime service he went to the Ransome and Marles Works Band, as its new principal cornet player (1946-1959). Back in those days Robert and James Scott seemed to follow each other around from one top band to another, and as Robert left Grimethorpe his place was taken by James for a short while before he went on to the Munn and Felton's Band.

James can remember the day he was given his Grimethorpe Colliery Band uniform. The tunic still had the name of the previous occupant in it, 'Robert Oughton'. James recalled that Robert was not known for being profligate in his ways, which was highlighted when James mentioned to Ray Craggs (one the band's bass players) that the leather tab that went under the hook and eyes of the choker collar was missing, to which Ray replied, 'That's because Bobby (Robert Oughton) cut the piece of leather out of the collar to cover a hole in the sole of his shoe ...'

Between 1935 and 1939 Robert was the Champion Cornet player of the North of England, with medals won at Derby in 1935, Leeds in 1936, Bury in 1938 and Oldham in 1939. These medals are now proudly displayed in the Dalmellington band bandroom.

During the war he served with the Scots Guards Band, but in 1945 he declined to sign on for another tour. However, he did sign on with the Royal Signals, and he was with the Royal Corps of Signals Band for two years, under the musical direction of Lieutenant Colonel Judd. In 1946 the Royal Signals Band was on tour in the United States of America. In the band at that time was Sir Alexander Gibson (1926-1995) who was then serving his compulsory National Service and later in life was the conductor of the Scottish National Symphony Orchestra.

At one of the Royal Signals' concerts Robert Oughton played the well-known cornet solo *Pandora* and as an encore he followed that with *Fairies on the Water*. Unbeknown to Robert, Raphael Mendez, the legendary principal trumpet player with the Metro Goldwyn Meyer Film Company Orchestra was in the audience. It is reported that (Sir) Alexander Gibson introduced Robert Oughton to Raphael, and over the years they became friends. This resulted in Robert Oughton acquiring some of the Mendez solos, and then re-arranging them with a brass band accompaniment. Some say they corresponded for many years afterwards, though there is no record of this in the Raphael Mendez archive in America.

Following his 'demob' day in 1947, Robert returned to the Dalmellington Band, but within three months he was back with Ransome and Marles. For the next twelve years many of the Mendez arrangements were used on the radio broadcasts and in concerts he performed throughout the country with the Ransome and Marles Band.

I recently acquired some of his old recordings on a reel-to-reel tape, and he was a showman indeed. He was still being the showman in 1972 when he played with the Dalmellington Band, and performed the *Post Horn Gallop* on a live television programme. He played the opening in the traditional manner, but finished it off to an amazed television audience with his mouthpiece attached to the hollow tube of a music stand.

In the early 1950s he was a member of the Harry Mortimer's 'All Stars Brass Band', which was a group of forty of the top brass band players in the country. Another cornet player who remembers those days with Bobby Oughton is Derek Garside, who was the principal cornet player for CWS (Manchester) Band for twenty-five years. Robert was about ten years older than Derek and was considered him to be one of the star players in the brass band world. In view of his seniority and the fact Derek was still one of the new boys in the 'All Stars Band', he rarely spoke to Robert unless he actually spoke to him first. Derek considered him to be a very good technical player. However, as a person he was considered to be rather aloof, and was a person who preferred his own company. He didn't really mix with everyone else, and was very much a private person.

It was 1964 when Robert first appeared on the big stage as a conductor as the musical director at the Scottish CWS Band. He conducted the band to qualification for the Royal Albert Hall National Championships. At a time when most conductors were still wearing the traditional conductor's uniform it has been said that Robert was the only conductor who conducted his bands wearing a lounge suit with white gloves, and was seen regularly wearing them at Whit Friday Contests.

In 1970 he was appointed the musical director of Carlton Main Frickley Colliery Band, a position he held for the next five years. While he took them to the Royal Albert Hall in both 1971 and 1973 and the British Open Championships from 1970 through to 1975, he was in the prizes only once. The band's best performance came on Saturday, 2 September 1972, at the Royal Albert Hall. The test piece was Jack Beaver's *Sovereign Heritage*. Playing off No. 16, the band was awarded second place behind the champions, Black Dyke Mills Band. One of those players in Carlton Main Frickley Colliery Band that day was the well known tuba soloist, conductor and adjudicator Steve Sykes, who has very happy memories of that day. He first met Robert Oughton in his early days of playing in the newly re-formed Carlton Main Frickley Colliery Junior Band, which Robert re-started. Steve's father Bill, who was colliery manager at Carlton back in those days, volunteered Steve to be one of the junior band's first members. The level of respect Robert received from all the young lads who joined that new band is high on his list of memories from those days.

It was whilst he was with Carlton Main that he probably played his last solo performance at the Coal Industry Social Welfare Organisation (CISWO) twenty-second Annual Yorkshire Festival in 1971. In 1976 Robert had moved back to Scotland and soon back at the Royal Albert Hall, having come full circle when he conducted the Dalmellington Band. Following the death of his father in 1961, he made his first visit to the Faroe Islands, and became involved with the Havnar Hornorkestur (Torshaven Band). Robert is still remembered there today. On Wednesday, 29 June 1995, Robert Oughton died, alone at his home in Forfar.

CECIL OUGHTON

Cecil was the youngest son of William and Violetta, and was born on the 6 February 1923 at 27 William Street, Hetton-le-hole. Along with his two brothers his childhood was spent at their new home at Dalmellington and went to Dalmellington High School (which has since been re-named Doon Academy). At the age of seven he was introduced to the cornet by his father, and was soon playing duets with his brother Robert.

Cecil 'Tiny' Oughton, who turned to dance band music, and went on to play for Nat Gonella and his Georgians.

As his playing began to mature his musical preference began to drift away from brass band music and brass bands, much against his father's wishes; this often caused friction within the family. Cecil had leanings towards the world of big bands, and as the arguments about this continued in the family, Cecil, without his father's knowledge, left home aged just fourteen. He found himself in Morecambe and the chance sight of an advertisement for a young trumpet player was to change his musical life for ever. The advertisement was for the Nat Gonella's new Georgians Dance Band. A successful audition followed and a new life began.

In those early days he was looked after by Nat Gonella's wife Stella Moya, who sang with the band, and after much persuading he told them where he came from. It was not long after that they contacted his father, who travelled down from Dalmellington to try and persuade his son to come back home, but Cecil had made his mind up that he wanted to stay. Nat Gonella realised he had a precocious talent on his hands and told his father that if he allowed Cecil to stay both he and his wife would look after him as if was their own son. William agreed that under those terms he could stay.

By 1939 the rift between father and son had been healed, so much so that he invited his father to Blackpool to watch one of the band's performances. You can imagine what William must have thought when he learned that Cecil was being paid £24 per week, a wage that William would have only dreamt of in those days. it was a busy life for a young teenager: Cecil and the band played at each venue Monday through to Saturday and then travelled on Sunday to the next venue.

The Gonella Band was now being heard regularly on BBC radio broadcasts, which both supplemented their income and gave them publicity that led to even more opportunities of performing live, in both the dance halls and theatres. Cecil, at 6ft 2in tall, was billed as 'Tiny Oughton, the virtuoso trumpeter and slide trumpet player'.

In 1942 Cecil was called up for compulsory war service in the Royal Artillery, and on the 2 July 1944 his parents received official notification that Cecil had been killed in action. At the time of his death, twenty-one-year-old Gunner 1116878 Cecil Oughton was a member of the 59th (6th Battalion, Hampshire Regiment) Royal Artillery Tank Regiment. The Allied offensive in North-Western Europe began with the Normandy landings on the 6 June 1944, and Cecil was killed in the fighting during the second week, when Caen was captured and the Allied forces were preparing their advance beyond the Seine. He was interred at Banneville-la-Campagne war cemetery, along with over 2,000 other Commonwealth Burials of the Second World War. One hundred and forty of them were unidentified, and five were Polish graves.

The name of Cecil Oughton lives on today in the form of two awards: one is a music trophy which is awarded annually at Doon Academy, and the second is for the annual Cecil Oughton Memorial Slow Melody Contest held by Dalmellington Band. This competition has recently celebrated its sixtieth year. This event is one of the highlights of Dalmellington Band's calendar and over the years has attracted many famous names from the world of brass bands to adjudicate the soloists and then to take part in the closing concert.

There are many families that have been associated with brass bands, but few who have had the same level of success as the Oughton family.

THE LAYCOCK FAMILY

I first came across the name of the St Hilda's Colliery Band and, more importantly to this story, the names of Arthur Laycock, and his brother Harold, as a young police constable in the old Leeds City Police, almost forty years ago. My regular patch back in those days included the large open market, with countless stalls. It was here where I saw one particular stall that was piled high with old 78s.

Whilst rummaging through some of these old records, I came across one in particular on the old Zonophone Record Label; on the one side it was a cornet solo *Titania*, played by Arthur Laycock, and on the other side the cornet duet *Ida and Dot*. Both recordings were accompanied by the St Hilda's Colliery Band. Even after I paid my 6*d* for the record I had no means of playing it (at the time I was living in digs in Leeds which did not run to having a record player of my own, let alone one that played 78s).

However, a few weeks after buying the record I did get a chance of playing it, and heard for the first time the phenomenal playing of someone who over the years was to become a musical hero of mine, the late Arthur Laycock. Over the years since I purchased that first record I have managed to find copies of all his solo recordings, dating back to 1913.

Arthur Laycock was born on 4 March 1887 and lived at 1 Hole Bottom, Stansfield, Todmorden, and was the second son of Thomas, a loom tackler in a local cotton mill, and Mary (*née* Sutcliffe) Laycock. He had three brothers: Ellis (b. 1875), William (b. 1892) and Harold (b. 1895).

I understand that both parents had died by 1910, and with no other adult relatives to look after the boys the parental responsibilities were taken on by their eldest brother Ellis, who remained a bachelor throughout his life. It is believed that both parents were interred in Hebden Bridge. Just how Arthur came to be involved in playing a brass instrument remains a mystery, as neither of his mother or his father appear to have been musically inclined, though Ellis played the concertina.

Shortly after his ninth birthday his parents bought Arthur a second-hand cornet, and arranged for him to see Arthur Hirst, the conductor of the local Cornholme Band, for some private lessons. This band was based at the Cornholme village on the outskirts of Todmorden,

Yours Sincerely, Arthur Laycock.

Left: *The St Hilda's Colliery Band at the Horsley Hill ground for a Cup tie in 1921. Arthur is fourth from the left on the back row. Harold is fourth from the right on the front row.*

Right: *Arthur and Harold relax together.*

and was quite successful. Its best result was at the Belle Vue September contest in 1893, when it was awarded second place. It is documented that Arthur made very good early progress, so much so that he was promoted on to the repiano cornet position. As his playing became even more proficient, and no doubt on the recommendation of Arthur Hirst, he was then given further tuition by George Nicholls, the highly respected solo cornet player with the Kingston Mills Band, and someone who lived quite close to young Arthur.

It was not long before he was invited to join the Todmorden Old Band as its new third cornet player, whilst still under the tuition of George Nicholls. Within three months he was promoted by Todmorden's bandmaster Chris Smith to be the repiano cornet player.

In 1904, at the age of seventeen, Arthur was once again recommended by George Nicholls, this time to the Hebburn Colliery Band some 135 miles away in the North East of England, as the new Assistant Principal Cornet player. However, soon after joining he was on his way back to the West Riding and rejoined Todmorden Old. He later joined the Earby Band under the baton of W. Rushton, and for a while would have played alongside the legendary (Foden's Band) cornet player Edwin Firth.

During this period he was approached by other bands about joining them. These included: the principal cornet position at Irwell Springs Band, which he declined; Wingates, to play with them for the Belle Vue and Crystal Palace contests, again declined. However, he did accept an offer from the Royal Oakley Band at Blaenau Festiniog, but at the first two contests the South Wales Brass Band Association disqualified him. In March 1909 he received an invitation to join the St Hilda's Colliery Band as its principal cornet player. At this time St Hilda's had been making steady progress, winning many local contests. Arthur's first success with the band came shortly after joining when it was placed first in the Grand Shield section at the Crystal Palace.

The number of individual contests entered by most bands a century ago was far more than any bands enter these days. As the contest calendar entered September the season was now in top gear, and although the band was entered in the Grand Shield Contest, and needed to practise relentlessly for that event, the band was still entered in another three contests before the big one. Following the success at the Crystal Palace in 1909, Arthur was invited to be a guest player with Besses o'th' Barn Band, which was about to embark on a round-the-world tour. Although the officials at Besses' tried to persuade him to join, he returned to St Hilda's in March 1911.

After winning the 1912 Championships at the Crystal Palace and becoming the national champions, the band began to record 78rpm records, and by the time the band closed down in 1937 it has produced about 300 recordings.

The Todmorden Orchestra, pre-1915. Harold Laycock is holding the tenor horn in the middle row, second from the left.

The musical career of Harold Laycock started not on a brass instrument but on the violin. In 1913, then aged seventeen, he decided that he wanted to play a brass instrument, and with a friend walked three miles to the Cornholme bandroom where he was able to hire the only instrument available, a tenor horn, for 2s 6d. He kept practicing, and when a vacancy did occur for a third horn player he was invited to join. He was later to leave and join the much more experienced Todmorden Old Band.

Following the death of the band's solo trombone player, Mr E. Kingsbury, in 1914, the bandmaster Walter Mitchell urged Harold to transfer onto the trombone. After only a few rehearsals he was being told, 'You'll make a player some day lad, stick with it.' In 1915 Harold began taking trombone lessons from Mr E.F. Woodhead, who had been the solo trombone player at Shaw band, Lancashire. Later that year Harold joined the 15th Battalion of the Worcester Regiment, and by June 1916 was in France serving as a stretcher bearer, but after only a few months he was sent back to the base with serious problems with his feet. He did rejoin his battalion later and continued his service. At the end of the war, whilst waiting for demobilisation at Harfleur, Normandy, he was attached to the 100th Infantry Brigade and was appointed the acting-bandmaster. His demobilisation came in October 1919. During his war service he met, just the once, Edwin Firth, the famous Foden's Works Band principal cornet player, who was in the London Regiment (Artist's Rifles), and was killed in June 1918 aged twenty-nine.

It was now that he joined his brother Arthur at St Hilda's Colliery Band on second trombone, sitting next to the famous trombone player Jimmy Southern. Harold's big opportunity on the solo trombone position came in 1920 at a contest in Glasgow (the test piece was *Tam O'Shanter*). William Halliwell, the band's famous professional conductor, moved him up on to the solo position because Jimmy was having denture trouble. From that day on he was confirmed as the band's new solo trombone player. Throughout his seven years with St Hilda's he won four Crystal Palace Championship medals, including three bars, and played at a Royal Command Performance at Buckingham Palace.

Harold left in January 1927, and joined the Callendar Cable Works Band in Erith, Kent. This band had by this time become one of the country's leading brass bands. Harold was given a job at the works as the factory site gateman. He was a member of this band for seventeen years, during which time he was involved in over 100 radio broadcasts and recorded several trombone solos.

In 1946 Harold returned to the North and was appointed the conductor of the Blackhall Colliery Band. In later years he held similar positions at a number of other bands which included: Blyth LNER, Forfar Instrumental, Windsor Colliery Workman's Silver in South Wales, Ovington Prize, Butterknowle Prize Silver, North Kent Silver and Dudley and Wallsend Borough. In his later years he was often seen on the contest adjudicator's circuit both locally and on the National Championship scene. He taught instrumental playing at schools in Northumberland. Harold died in 1974. Following his death many of his contemporaries described him as, 'The Caruso of the Trombone' and 'the Prince of Soloists'.

On Wednesday, 9 February 1921, the St Hilda's Colliery Band was commanded by the King to perform at Buckingham Palace. Arthur Laycock played William Rimmer's cornet solo, *Titania*, a performance that was particularly commended by Their Majesties. The Queen remarked, 'I was delighted at the beautiful cornet solo.' Again, at the Command Performance at Lambton Castle a great personal compliment was paid to Arthur Laycock when the King sent intimation that he was coming to hear him perform *Rule Britannia*. Shortly afterwards His Majesty came into the hall and took his place by the side of his Royal Consort, remaining in the hall until the end of the performance, and said how delighted he had been with the playing.

Arthur was a member of St Hilda's for fourteen years, and it was widely regarded that a great deal of the band's success was due to his untiring efforts. In 1923, his last concert with St Hilda's was at the Finsbury Park Empire when he left the band to join the Eastbourne Municipal Orchestra, under its conductor Captain Harry G. Amers. He was someone who he played under during his wartime days with the Northumberland Hussars. He played with the orchestra for three years, but in 1926 he left Eastbourne with what was described as an infection of the heart, having earlier spent several months in a London nursing home after a nervous breakdown. Finally, he joined Frank Gomez, who was the musical director at the Whitby Municipal Orchestra, and played with this orchestra for two seasons.

Throughout this time he was in constant demand as a soloist and regularly performed as the guest soloist for bands throughout the country, and was regarded as being one of the most successful brass recording artist of his time. In 1929 his old friend E.F. Woodhead who was the musical director of the St Austell Town Band, Cornwall, invited Arthur to be the guest soloist at two concerts on Sunday 27 January. It was reported in the *Royal Cornwall Gazette & News* that on his arrival at St Austell he was already ill with flu. Being the true professional his appearance at the two concerts went ahead. On the Monday he was confined to his bed and the local doctor attended him and was diagnosed with bronchopneumonia. He was looked after by a nurse day and night. Over the next few days his illness fluctuated from being a bit better to being really poorly. On the Thursday he was described as being dangerously ill, and such was the concern about his health that a telegram was sent to his wife and to his brother Harold at Callender's Cable Works in Erith Kent. By the Monday, pleurisy was also a problem for him. He died on Tuesday, 5 February 1929.

The following day he was conveyed the 400 miles back to Earby. The funeral took place on Saturday 9 February at Thornton Church (All Saints) in Earby, and was attended by all the well-known names in the brass band world, and was reportedly one of the largest funerals seen in the area for many years.

[Harold] won many prizes. His greatest memory, and the one he treasured most, was the winning of a gold medal and his beating of Harry Mortimer into second prize with his performance of *Lend Me Your Aid* and [Harry's performance of] *Softly Awakes My Heart*. He was considered virtually unbeatable on slow melody.

He was a stalwart of the brass band movement, a truly great player and artist and a life-long enthusiast, and my never-to-be-forgotten dear friend.

Robert (Bob) Wray, Sunderland, an acknowledged expert on the St Hilda's Colliery Band

THE MIDGLEY FAMILY

One of the nicest things about contributing to the *British Bandsman* is the feedback I receive from readers. These come in the form of e-mails, telephone calls and some very interesting letters.

One letter I received was from Margaret Midgley (*née* Keeys). Margaret was brought up in the Salvation Army and was from a musical family. From early childhood her life was surrounded by music and musicians. In 1965 she married Jack Midgley, a fine trombone player who was held in high esteem in and around the Durham County Brass Band League. Margaret first met Jack by chance when he asked if she would be his accompanist at a local church concert. His usual accompanist was unavailable, and, having struggled to find someone else, the situation was getting desperate. As the concert date drew nearer something had to be done or the concert would have to be cancelled. Margaret followed in her mother's footsteps as a pianist and started having lessons when she was only six years old, and by the time Jack asked her she was quite capable. It was his mother who suggested that he should ask Margaret because, as the SA Songster and Corps' pianist, she was quite used to accompanying brass. Although Margaret did not know him personally, she knew of him, having seen his photograph in the local newspaper many times after he had won yet another solo competition.

Jack was born in 1920 in Hartlepool, and was one of the four children of Herbert and Elizabeth Midgley, who were members of the local Salvation Army. Margaret says they were a truly musical family with all of them playing a brass instrument. In Jack's case it was initially the tenor horn.

In 1926 the Midgley family left the Salvation Army and formed their own West Hartlepool Mission Silver Prize Band. Clifford was on cornet, Jack on solo trombone, Joy on solo horn (who had joined in 1934); Stan Sykes on solo euphonium, Mr Midgley, Snr, played bass, Mrs Midgley played the cornet part, and Clifford and Edith played the baritone. This family mission band was kept busy performing in over 100 concerts.

Left to right: Clifford, band master and cornet player; Mrs Midgley, cornet; Joy, horn; Edith, baritone; Stan Sykes, solo euphonium (he was Edith's husband); Jack, solo trombone; and Mr Midgley on bass.

Jack Midgley in 1936.

It was Mr Midgley Snr who formed the Hartlepool Public Prize Band from the mission band, and for a number of years the band did well under the baton of Clifford. Successes included Durham County League Area Champions in 1943, and second prize in the second section, *Daily Herald* Northern area contest in 1947. This local band was seen regularly in Hartlepool's Ward Jackson Park.

Jack started playing at the age of seven and joined the family's West Hartlepool Mission Silver Prize Band two years later, playing the tenor horn. While he was playing the tenor horn he was also playing about with a trombone, and in 1934 he gave up playing the tenor horn and joined the band's trombone section. This was to be his instrument for the rest of his life. In 1935 he entered his first solo competition and won the junior section. His family and friends could see that he had talent as a trombone player, and it was suggested that he took lessons from one of the best trombone players of his generation, Harold Laycock.

These lessons saw Jack come on in leaps and bounds. Between 1935 and 1939 he won eighteen solo competitions, gaining ten firsts, four seconds and four thirds. These solo competitions were held throughout the North of England, and so his reputation as a good player was beginning to be recognised far beyond his own community.

At the National Festival Finals of 1936, the last to be held at the Crystal Palace, he was the principal trombone player at Thornley Colliery Band under the baton of Edward Kitto. That year the band played in the Junior Cup 'A' section. This was also the year the Crystal Palace burnt down, a far more memorable event than Thornley not being in the prizes for that last visit to the glass palace. Over seventy years have gone by since that day and means that there are fewer surviving players around today who can say they played at that magnificent venue.

In 1936 a British Boys' Band (I would be pleased to hear from readers who know anything about this band) was being formed to tour South Africa. Jack was invited to take part. However, his father intercepted the letter and decided that he was too young. He was not told about the invitation until many years later.

In 1937 he won both the junior and senior solo contests at Hebburn-on-Tyne, which led to him being invited for an audition at the BBC. However, the BBC sent a follow-up letter saying they had decided that they felt the trombone was not a suitable instrument for broadcasting.

His growing reputation was brought to the attention of Jack Atherton, who invited him to join the famous Harton Colliery Band, which he was conducting at that time. It was as a member of this band that he would get to know some of the most well-known names in brass bands at the time, such as Norman Ashcroft, Norman Piper, Maurice Murphy, Jimmy Kay and Sidney Poole. Jimmy who wrote the march 'Queensbury', which was and still is the signature tune of Black Dyke. Jack first met Jimmy when the band was playing at Morecambe. Jimmy asked the band secretary if he could share a room with a bandsman that did not smoke or drink. It was arranged that he would share with Jack – but what they did not know was that Jack was prone to sleep walking! Jimmy barely lasted one night before he asked for a move.

This was the time of the Second World War and getting to band rehearsals was very difficult. Rehearsals were every Tuesday and Thursday evenings, and were extended to also include all day Saturday and Sunday. With three live broadcasts every month from the BBC studios in Newcastle, every member had to be there and dared not miss it or they were out.

The band took part in all the major contests and along with many of the top bands of that time was booked to perform at a number of seaside resorts for a week throughout the summer months, which meant three different programmes were performed daily. At the end of the war Jack left Harton due to business commitments and the difficulty he had in travelling to South Shields for all the rehearsals.

In 1946 Jack was awarded fourth prize at the *Daily Herald* North of England Area Championship Solo Contest in Bradford. He was in good company that day, with Ernest Appleyard, who went on to play with Brighouse and Rastrick, taking the first prize; Frank Wesson, Hickleton Main, second place, and E.F. O'Grady of Bullcroft St John's Ambulance Band coming in third. The following year at the same contest, which was held in Gateshead, Jack was awarded first place in the trombone section with 185 points, (fourth overall in the whole event). The runner-up that year was Lance Winn with 165 marks and he went on to play with Black Dyke Mills Band. Following his success at this contest Jack was approached by Brighouse and Rastrick Band to play principal trombone under Eric Ball, but owing to business commitments he had to decline the offer.

Mr Midgley, Snr went on to be a leading official in the Durham League for many years and presented the League with one of its first trophies. Following his death, Jack and Clifford, along with Stan Sykes, joined the Head Wrightson Works Band, with Clifford as the band's musical director. This band in a period of six years from 1955 to 1960 shot up from the fouth section to become a championship section band.

The Head Wrightson Works Band went through a number of name changes. Today it is the successful Lockwood Brass, based in Lingdale, East Cleveland. Even though Jack settled in at Head Wrightson, he was still in demand. In 1958 Professor Walter Hargreaves asked him personally if he would join Crookhall Colliery Band, and whilst he was very pleased to be asked, he was happy to stay with his friends and colleagues at the Head Wrightson Works Band.

From left to right: Herbert, Joy, Jack, Edith, Clifford and Elizabeth Midgley.

I knew Jack for more than thirty years as a personal friend and previously as a player at the Head Wrightson Works Band and later at Yarm and District Band, where he was a fine trombonist and band manager. When I was elected chairman of the then Durham County Brass Band League in 1985, Jack was the vice president, and he gave me his full support then and his close friendship from those days. When I felt I needed advice, Jack never failed me.

In November 1992 in the county council chambers in Durham a band of about 320 volunteer players from a number of bands, all dressed in their respective band uniforms, presented a concert to the full council and supporters from throughout the county. Jack brought his wife Margaret, who was persuaded to sit in the balcony alongside Tom Finkel, the League's president. That event was the highlight of my period in office as chairman and without the support of Jack Midgley it may not have happened at all.

Both Jack and Margaret have been loyal to the brass band movement in the Durham area ... His memory still lives on in the form of a 'Best Trombone' trophy which is presented annually to the best trombone player in section A of the annual association contest.

George Bamfitt, president of the Durham County Brass Band League

Clifford's son Brian, who became a fine trombone player in his own right, was also a member of a highly successful trombone quartet formed by Jack and Clifford. Clifford was on 'G' trombone, Stan Sykes on third, Brian on second and Jack on solo. The quartet's greatest success came when they were placed second in the British Quartet Championships.

I am sure many of the older Middlesborough FC supporters will still remember the band back in the club's Ayresome Park days. Clifford's *Post Horn Gallop* was a party-piece solo that the supporters encored many times, along with Jack's superb slippery slide solos.

Jack hung his trombone up and finished playing with the band when he reached the age of seventy-five, but with banding in his blood he continued working for the band as the band secretary, and as a vice president for the Durham County Brass Band League. On 21 February 2003, aged eighty-two, Jack died after a brief spell in hospital. He was a quality trombone player, winning more solo competitions than most others. He played solo trombone for Harton Colliery, Head Wrightson and with Horden Colliery, all three very prestigious bands in the North East. He dedicated his life to banding.

Margaret says that Jack was a modest man about his musical achievements. One of the things she wanted to do was to display his solo contest medals in a frame on the wall. However, Jack's modesty prevailed, if only for a while. Margaret finally got her way but when they were mounted and proudly put on display Jack always wanted to take them down when they were to have visitors.

Just some of the many medals and cups won by Jack Midgley, a quiet, unassuming man who did his talking with his trombone.

4

FROM PLAYER TO CONDUCTOR

Brighouse and Rastrick Band in 1929. Members included: Fred Berry, J. Vernon Lister,
F. Haigh, Wilf Swingler, G. Murray, Frank Wilby, Harold Swallow, Jim France, J. Broomhead,
D. Seed, Charles Badrock, Bertie Groves, Sam Rushworth, W.B. Sykes, Tom Wilby, Wilfred
France, Victor France, Milnes Wood, Ronnie Fawthrop, Jimmy Squires, John Beaumont,
H.E. Dyson, W.F. Shackleton, Ernest White, R. Seed.

FRED BERRY

'A great player and a wonderful band trainer'

Fred Berry was one of the finest band trainers of all time. He was born in Honley, a small village on the outskirts of Huddersfield, and joined the Honley Band as a junior instrumentalist. He became one of the best euphonium players in the country. After a short time at Linthwaite Band, in 1898 he transferred to the successful Wyke Temperance Band. In 1906 he joined the famous Besses o'th' Barn Band, and went on its eighteen-month world tour, and then a Canadian tour in 1912.

In 1910 he conducted Clifton Band to third place in the Crystal Palace Junior Cup, and the following year he took the band to second place in the same competition. The final winner was decided on the toss of coin, as Clifton and Lincoln Malleable Band had been awarded the same number of points.

Having left Clifton he accepted the invitation to join Brighouse. In July 1929 he conducted the band to first place at Belle Vue, playing Henry Geehl's test piece *Oliver Cromwell*. While this was a tremendous feat for the band, little did the members know the success that was about to come. In the September contest at Belle Vue, a contest now called the British Open Championship, once again under the baton of Fred Berry, the band was awarded first place, playing Beethoven's *Pathetique Symphony*. Only one other band had achieved the Belle Vue double before (Batley Old in 1890), and it stunned the band world.

Fred took the band to Belle Vue in 1930 and '31 but was unplaced, and then in 1932 the band employed the services of professional conductor William Halliwell. He was the conductor who, it was said, had waved a golden baton from 1910. The band completed a hat-trick of wins at the September Belle Vue Contest with William, and won again in 1936. There was reportedly a row after the 1929 win because the band wanted a professional conductor, so Fred stood aside to allow William to take over for the 1932 contest. Fred never conducted at a contest again, however, in the annals of the Brighouse and Rastrick Band, he is a legend.

I recall in 1953 the band had been asked to play at the Barnsley Co-op Hall at one of its Saturday night brass band concerts. The band's conductor, John Harrison, was unable to attend this engagement, and Fred Berry stepped in to conduct the band at the last minute. Then in his eighties, this was the last time he conducted any band, and sadly he died the following Wednesday [20 May 1953]. He was a great player and a wonderful band trainer.
Frank Longbottom, member of Brighouse and Rastrick Band from 1949 to 1963

KENNETH DENNISON

'Always very professional in his approach to music'

Kenneth Dennison's life in music began in Rothwell, a town on the outskirts of Leeds, back in the days when (including the surrounding villages), the whole area could boast six fully subscribed brass bands.

His introduction into brass bands came as a six-year-old schoolboy when he was taken to listen to the rehearsals of the Rothwell Temperance Band. This was in 1937, the same year the band took part in the Belle Vue September Contest playing Dennis Wright's arrangement of the *Academic Festival Overture*. Little did young Kenneth know that he too would perform at this contest in the future.

The Second World War affected all the local brass bands. Rothwell Temperance even called in the uniforms and instruments. In 1941 the band committee realised the potential of forming a new band from the youngsters. Advertising locally, the committee attracted quite a number of interested people. From all the applicants, a final twenty-six were selected, with an average age of eleven years old, Kenneth was lucky enough to be given a cornet. After only a short while, Kenneth achieved his first musical ambition by changing his instrument to a trombone. The boys were all encouraged to have private tuition and Kenneth was fortunate to have the opportunity of taking his lessons with Ernest Appleyard, a well-known and respected trombonist who played with Brighouse and Rastrick Band.

In 1943 it was felt the band had made sufficient progress to enter its first contest, which was at Odsal Stadium, a sporting venue which is better known these days as the home of Bradford Bulls rugby league club. The band came second, a wonderful start – though it is slightly less impressive when you discover that only two bands took part!

With regular rehearsals on Tuesday and Thursday evenings and Sunday afternoons, the band entered its next contest in 1944 at Bradford's Eastbrook Hall, with a higher sense of optimism. The lads did well, coming second in one section and winners in the main event. For the next four years they were awarded seven first and nine second prizes. As well as Kenneth, the band's members included Derrick Ward (who went on to be a junior cornet champion and a member of Brighouse and Rastrick), and Gordon Roberts on euphonium, another future solo junior champion, so the band was sure of a bright future. Looking back to his early playing days, Kenneth singles out Mr Newton and Mr Appleyard as the two people who helped him through the first step of his life in music.

In 1946, then aged sixteen, Kenneth was very pleased to win the prestigious Alexander Owen Memorial Scholarship.

In 1949 he received his call-up papers for his National Service and joined the Central Band of the RAF. He not only enjoyed it, but gained valuable musical experience. The style of playing was different from his days back in Rothwell, and the balance of brass with the

Left to right: Ernest Appleyard, trombone player with Brighouse and Rastrick Band; Campbell Holmes, the Australian second trombone player in his Ferodo Works Band uniform; and Kenneth Dennison, trombone player with Fairey Aviation Works Band. The three musicians were caught on camera during a break at the September Contest at Belle Vue.

woodwind had to be understood. During his National Service he was also able to gain quite a lot of conducting experience, which helped him greatly in his later years. He was very tempted to stay in the RAF, but a totally unexpected telephone call changed all that; the telephone call came from none other than Harry Mortimer, who invited him to join the Fairey Aviation Works Band at Stockport.

Kenneth joined the band on first trombone in July 1951. He still had some military service to complete, but – possibly through the intervention of 'HM' – he suddenly found that he had been given leave to perform at all Fairey's engagements, the only proviso being that he returned to RAF Uxbridge every second Thursday, to be paid.

His first engagement with the band was on Monday 16 July, playing for *Music While You Work* at the BBC studio at the Playhouse Theatre, in London. It was then straight to the Alexandra Palace to prepare for a live broadcast on BBC television. The broadcast finished late in the evening, but the band had a hectic schedule in those days. No sooner had the broadcast finished than the band was on its way to Worthing for a whole week of daily performances, and sometimes a twice-daily concert.

With so many engagements it was vital that everyone got on with each other. Kenneth recalls the band was never put up in the 'Hotel de Posh', but just in ordinary 'digs', where there would often be five or six members in one household. This produced a togetherness which was reflected in every performance, with everyone being loyal to the band and to each other.

Kenneth, like everyone else in the band, was found a job at the Heaton Chapel factory. It worked out pretty well for him: he was given a position in the personnel department, and his boss was the band manager. These were exciting times: concerts every week, BBC broadcasts, tours (including two visits to Canada, which included a month at the Canadian National Exhibition in 1961, and ten days at Niagara Falls in 1972). A lot of notes were played in a two-hour concert programme, twice a day and a minimum of fourteen in a week. As a soloist you were expected to 'stand up' at least once every day. Whilst this was heavy going, you have to remember that the band was not playing 'heavy works', although occasionally, a forthcoming test piece would be slipped into the programme to give it an airing. This was usually given under another title: for example, at one concert in 1970 at Hyde Park, *Cortege* from Herbert Howell's wonderful piece *Pageantry* became the middle movement of *Pineapple Poll*.

When the band was crowned 'National Champions' it would be engaged to play at the big northern agricultural shows such as Stokesley and Bishop Auckland. It was about the only time bands such as Fairey's would ever march in a procession followed by carts which displayed produce, cows, horses and goats. Judging from the neighs and moos, Kenneth could never make his mind up whether they liked *Knight Templar* or not.

Filling a vacancy today can be very difficult, but in the old days Kenneth recalls that the membership of Fairey's and many of the other bigger named bands remained fairly static, which gave long-term continuity. The trombone section is a prime example, with Kenneth on first trombone, Frank Clayton on second and Arnold Hall on bass trombone for seventeen years. During Kenneth's twenty-five years there were only three principal solo cornets – Norman Ashcroft, Philip McCann and Kevin Bolton – and there were only two solo euphonium players in the same period – Harry Cheshire and Marcus Cutts.

Contesting was always special during Kenneth's era at Fairey's, with a real purple patch during the early 1960s at both Belle Vue and the National Finals at the Royal Albert Hall. Of all the successes, Kenneth's most memorable was the National Championship performance in 1956. The test piece was Eric Ball's *Festival Music*, playing off No. 15 under the baton of Major George Willcocks. The band was placed first, two points clear of CWS (Manchester) Band. The band had already won the British Open Championship playing Denis Wright's *Tam O'Shanter's Ride* with H.M. and the 1963 British Open win playing *Life Divine* to complete the hat-trick.

The band rehearsed every Tuesday and Thursday after work and every Friday lunchtime in the works' canteen. Kenneth remembers the reaction of the staff in the canteen: when the band had finished playing a piece, all the staff would applaud by tapping their rice pudding plates with a knife. Having been the band manager since 1957, Kenneth was appointed the musical director following the death of Leonard Lamb in 1968. This marked the end of his trombone-playing days. During his time as musical director the band produced eight new LP records, came second twice at the World Championships, and won the 1972 Wills Brass Band Championships and the BBC series *Champion Brass* in 1976.

Kenneth's career with Fairey's came to an end that same year because he changed jobs. He moved into teaching, and served as the musical director of Mirrlees Band in Stockport and the City of Coventry Band. In 1978 he was awarded a well-deserved silver medal from the Worshipful

I became a member of the Fairey Aviation Works Band in the summer of 1956, and I soon realised that Kenneth Dennison was a very fine leader of a trombone section that eventually played together as a team for seventeen years. Kenneth was a very expressive player who could interpret the music as the composer intended. He eventually became the band's manager, a job he carried out with a high degree of competence and fairness during some difficult times for the band. During his time as music director the band gave many fine concerts throughout Great Britain and also in Canada ... It was during this period that we achieved what must be a record, by playing at Folkestone for consecutive weeks including two concerts per day without repeating one piece of music.

Kenneth always took pride in his appearance and was always very professional in his approach to music. We still keep in touch and ring each other to chat about our times together at Fairey's.

Alan Lawton MBE, who was a front-row cornet player for twenty years, band manager for ten years and eight years as the Fairey Band's resident conductor

The Fairey Band in 1973 at the Stockport Town Hall. From left to right, back row: Eric Bratt, Tony Cresswell, John Tucker, Frank Grocott, Cyril Howarth, Frank Clayton, Harry Foster and Alf Morton. Third row: Barry Hinde, Norman Ashcroft, Jack Hewitt, Tom Fielding, Marcus Cutts. Second row: Colin Mannion, Albert Fletcher, Ken Squires, Ray Peacock, Denis Dawson, Roy Garlick, Cliff Colwell and Doug Pritchard. Front row: Colin Waggott, Alan Lawton, Kenneth Dennison, Bert Howarth and Philip McCann.

In October 1965, Leonard Lamb achieved the hat-trick with Fairey's in 1961, 1962 and 1963, and then showed everyone that he was something very special by winning it again with them in 1965.

Company of Musicians of the City of London for his services to brass bands. Musically he was in regular demand as an adjudicator, and once he established himself in the South West he helped several bands, which included Thornbury near Bristol, and Torrington and Sidmouth bands in Devon. He now lives in Putney and is still involved with brass bands, including his association with the Mid-Sussex Band Burgess Hill, as an advisor. Up until quite recently he had served for fifteen years as the president of the Southern Counties Amateur Brass Band Association. On reflection, he says there have been many exciting moments in his sixty-six years of banding, and hopes that he has been able to make some small contribution to the general good.

JOSEPH C. DYSON

'This was my real start, and right well I did too'

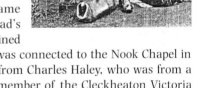

On Friday, 23 December 1945, the Golders Green Cemetery in London witnessed one of its largest gatherings for many years. Among the gathered throng were musicians, conductors, composers, and administrators from the world of brass bands. The BBC and the London County Council was also represented. They were all there to pay their last respects to Joseph C. Dyson, someone who for over fifty years had enjoyed a successful career both as a cornet player and a brass band conductor.

Joe, as he was known, was born in February 1883 at Low Spen, Gomersal, a small village between Halifax and Leeds, and came from a non-musical family. He was the second son of Roland and Emma Dyson. By the time he was eight years old his mother was a widow and was bringing up seven children on her own.

Joe's introduction to playing a brass instrument came when he became a member of the Gomersal Church Lad's Brigade, and played the bugle. As a twelve year old he joined the Cleckheaton Temperance Band, which at that time was connected to the Nook Chapel in Cleckheaton. In his early playing days he took lessons from Charles Haley, who was from a noted musical family in the area, and a distinguished member of the Cleckheaton Victoria band. Here we had a small town with two bands, neither of which exist today.

The Cleckheaton Victoria band came to prominence when it was awarded sixth place at the Crystal Palace, under the baton of Angus Holden in 1903. However, although it took part in the Crystal Palace contests on four further occasions before the First World War, the band never achieved the same level of placing again and then appears to have faded into history.

It was during the tenure of Angus Holden that Joe was persuaded to join the Victoria Band on soprano, a position he held for less than a year before he decided to leave and return to playing the cornet. It is recorded that Joe only ever had one lesson from a professional musician, and that was with Johnny Martin, an old local cornet player; it cost him 5s.

Once the Nook Chapel Band broke away from the chapel, it then became the Cleckheaton Temperance Band, and it was then that he got his first opportunity at conducting. This opportunity became a full-time position following the announcement by the regular conductor that he was leaving. During those early days of his conducting career with the Temperance band he also played solo cornet at the Wyke Temperance Band. From available records, although a little vague, it appears that at some point he also played with Black Dyke Mills and then at Wingates Temperance Band.

One of his earliest appearances as a solo cornet player at the Belle Vue September Contest was in 1907 with Batley Old, and then in 1909 with Lindley, 1912 with Wingates Temperance and finally in 1913 with Bentley Colliery (Doncaster). On that evidence he was certainly no slouch when it came to cornet playing, being in constant demand by many of the prominent bands in Yorkshire. Throughout this time he was also involved with many local orchestras, including the Cleckheaton Philharmonic, Brighouse Orchestra Society and others in Leeds, Bradford, Huddersfield, and he was even engaged on occasions as an extra cornet player for the Hallé Orchestra.

After the 1913 September Contest he was appointed the conductor of Brighouse and Rastrick Temperance Band (the Temperance part of their name had been dropped by 1929). On 27 September 1913, Joe conducted the band at what was its first taste of the big time at the National Brass Band Festival at the Crystal Palace. Playing Percy Fletcher's *Labour and Love*, what was then the first original piece of music written for contesting brass bands, the band played No. 10 and was awarded fifth place. The band's winnings for that effort amounted to £13 and a new cornet. Joe said after that memorable trip to the Crystal Palace, 'This was my real start, and right well I did.'

After the South Moor Colliery Band had won the Grand Shield on 28 September 1907 it was all set to become one of the top bands in the Durham area. The year 1908 was the band's first year in the top flight and they had the opportunity to perform at the Crystal Palace under the baton of William Heap, but it failed to meet everyone's expectations. For the next four years the band was conducted by Angus Holden, and with two sixth places the band was doing well. J.A. Greenwood was given the job in 1913, but the band again failed to make its mark. With no Crystal Palace contests held throughout the duration of the First World War, Joe's opportunity to conduct South Moor at the National Brass Band Festival came in 1921. The band went on to play at the Crystal Palace each year to 1928 but even with Joe at the helm the band could only manage a third place in 1925. The last time South Moor played at the London Finals was 1929 under the baton of Gus Haigh, and following this disappointing performance it seemed to draw to a close South Moor's flirtation with top-flight banding.

Before Joe moved to pastures new in southern England, here are just some of the bands he conducted (whilst he was not as successful at the highest level of competition, he did lead many of these bands to win numerous prizes at local competitions): Brighouse, Batley Old, Spenborough, Birstall, Lindley, Holme, Hinchliffe Mills, Meltham Mills, Slaithwaite, Marsden, Ravensthorpe, Thornhill, Ossett, Wakefield, Bradford City, Shipley, Rothwell Temperance, Friendly Subscription, South Moor Colliery, Backworth Colliery, Hetton Colliery, Horden Colliery and a number of other bands in the Durham and southern Scottish areas.

The South Moor Colliery Band, 1923. Joe is seated in the middle of the front row.

Above and right: *These two rather battered photographs are both extremely rare. The picture above shows the Hanwell Band on 29 December 1935 at the Prince of Wales theatre (the band gave two performances), while the picture on the right shows Cleckheaton Temperance Band.*

My father sent me for cornet lessons with Mr Dyson in the early 1930s when I was between eleven and twelve years old. The weekly one-hour lessons cost 5s. After each lesson he set me a list of the studies from the Arban tutor book and the scales he wanted me to practice for the following week.

The only contemporaries who were also having lessons at the same time were Eric Bravington, who went on to play the first trumpet in the London Philharmonic Orchestra, his cousin Arthur Wilkinson, who played with the Jack Hylton Dance Band and became a quite well-known arranger after the Second World War, and, on my dad's recommendation, Roland Cobb, who went on to become the greatly revered principal cornet player with the International Staff Band of the Salvation Army during the 1960s, under Lt-Col Bernard Adams.

'J.C.' had two sons who were in the Grenadier Guards Band, Fred (oboe and violin) and Rowland (cornet); both went on to be professional musicians with London orchestras after their military service.

'J.C.' also trained many other bands in the London area in addition to Hanwell. These included Northfleet, John Dickinson's and the Fire Brigade Band in Ealing. I recall meeting him in the Alexander Palace and he was in a great hurry because he had to conduct two bands drawn close together in the same contest but in different halls.

Bram Wiggins, ARAM, IRAM, ARCM, LTCL, composer and the former assistant first trumpet LSO

In 1929, Joe went to audition for the professional conductor's position at Hanwell Silver Band, and was one of sixty applicants for the post. Hanwell band committee felt it was time to have a regular conductor rather than a visiting professional, and Joe was the successful applicant. A cartoon in the local press commented on him being left handed, saying his right hand would be too busy collecting awards. When he arrived at Hanwell the committee gave him free rein in the musical running of the band, and under his direction it quickly became one of the foremost bands in the country.

On 29 December 1935 the Hanwell Band, conducted by Joe, was the first brass band to play in the West End at the Prince of Wales theatre. The band gave two performances. It was extremely busy with many prestigious concerts, and gradually began to win regular prizes on the contest scene as well. Although the band did not win at the highest level, Joe conducted the band during the 1930s at the Crystal Palace, Alexandra Palace and Belle Vue. The band's progress throughout this period was attributed to his hard work, and was considered as a turning point in the band's fortunes. He set a bench mark for the band's future. From being placed second at the Royal Albert Hall in 1950 with a new conductor George Thompson (later of Grimethorpe Colliery Band fame) Hanwell went on to take part in the National Championships through the 1960s and '70s under the baton of Eric Bravington.

Throughout Joe's musical career he was in regular demand as a band contest adjudicator. In 1938 he returned to his native Cleckheaton to adjudicate the local contest. This was his first trip back to his home town in forty years. It was here where it all started, when in 1911 he was offered the job and retainer of £10 per year as the conductor of the Cleckheaton Temperance Band.

Throughout his playing career he played under all the brass band conducting legends: John Gladney, Edwin Swift, William Rimmer, William Halliwell, Alf Gray and Angus Holden. Through their influence he came to be a highly respected brass band trainer.

There is little information available of Joe's own family except to say that he had two sons: Fred, who throughout his adult life lived in South Moor, County Durham, and Rowland, who was a cornet player, and was initially taught by his father until he joined the Grenadier Guards at fifteen. Rowland spent his later years in Hove, Sussex. Joe did have a younger brother, Luther, who also became a brass band conductor and for a number of years was at Clifton and Lightcliffe Band near Brighouse.

It was reported in the *British Bandsman* on 5 January 1945 that Harry Mortimer, who was representing the BBC, said after the funeral, 'Joe's cornet solo contesting days were back in a time of quite a school of outstanding players, and he was always in the first three.' It was also announced after the funeral that a solo contest challenge trophy would be given to perpetuate his memory. I wonder what happened to that trophy?

The well-known euphonium player Charley Brighton has produced a very interesting and helpful history of the Hanwell Band on his website www.euph9.freeserve.co.uk (click on the euphonium image and follow the link in the contents section).

Coda . . .

• J.C. Dyson paid his first visit as professional conductor to the Rothwell Temperance Band, near Leeds. His fee was 10s 6d each visit plus railway fare, but activities were subdued during the First World War.

• In 1930, the Tadley Band near Reading appointed Mr Joseph Dyson as a trainer. His wide experience as conductor to some of the top bands in contesting, broadcasting and recording was well known in the band world and it was fortunate that he had lately come to London from Yorkshire to carry on his work as a teacher and so was within easy travelling distance of Tadley. He was a master of technique, and with his skilful tuition and the co-operation of John Lambden, the Band were welded into a team and progress was notable and consistent.

• J.C. Dyson was one of the three adjudicators (along with Frank Wright and Dr Harold C. Hind) to officiate at the British Open Brass Band Championships in 1945.

ARTHUR O. PEARCE

'The Prime Minister of bandmasters'

Elderly gentlemen lined the streets and doffed their hats in the pouring rain and heavy sleet, as an expression of respect for a man many of them had known since childhood. Women stood and grasped their prams, pausing momentarily for a few moment's reflection on the icy pavements. They all stood transfixed at the sight of the cortége of one of the brass band world's most famous sons, a man known by many as the 'Prime Minister of Bandmasters'. Everyone looked on with quiet dignity as the funeral procession of the legendary Arthur Oakes Pearce passed through the hill-top village of Queensbury, the home of the famous and his beloved Black Dyke Mills Band, following his death on Saturday, 13 January 1951, at the age of seventy-nine.

Arthur Oakes Pearce was one of twelve children and was born on the 16 October 1871 at Lupset Park, Thornes Alverthorpe near Wakefield, and was the son of Peter and Caroline Pearce (*née* Oakes). Whether it was Peter Pearce's employment as a gardener that forced him and his family to move away from Wakefield to seek work elsewhere is a story that has long since been lost in the mists of time. However, it was shortly after Arthur had reached his twelfth birthday that the family had packed up and moved house out of the area. Little did young Arthur or his family know how it was going to change his life and ultimate destiny.

He came from a musical family, two of his brothers being horn players. His own introduction to the band world began a year later, shortly after his thirteenth birthday, when he took up playing an old side drum for the Bethel New Connexion Band at Ovenden in the Yorkshire mill town of Halifax, their new home. Becoming quite proficient, he left this band to join the Halifax Band of Hope, which went on to become the Halifax Victoria Band.

After a short while the band committee began to notice young Arthur's enthusiasm and desire to do well. This resulted in him being given what was considered to be a promotion back in those days, a move from playing the side drum to playing the baritone. By this time he was coming on in leaps and bounds, and once again promotion was not far off. The band's officials described him as a 'promising instrumentalist', and he found himself as the band's new solo horn player.

His baptism into the contesting world came as the solo horn player when the Halifax Temperance Band performed its test piece *St Paul* at the local skating rink. The band was awarded second prize, and the judge's remarks included a special mention of the solo horn player. Even in these early days, Arthur O. Pearce was being noticed. He stayed with the Temperance Band until he was twenty, with his final year being spent as the band's soprano cornet player.

His introduction to conducting came when he left the Temperance Band to join Copley Mills Brass Band as principal cornet player, another local band on the outskirts of Halifax, which

Brighouse and Rastrick Temperance Band in 1902. From left to right, back row: W.M. Barraclough, H. Crowther, J.L. Dyson, J.H. Hardy, M. Findlater, H. Slater, T. Jagger, S. Crowther, H. Nuttall, J. Squire, H. Rushton and W. Robinson. Front row: B. Robinson, F. Firth (treasurer), J. Tarlton, Arthur Oakes Pearce, H.E. Dyson (secretary), E. Ripley, Harry Hodgson (conductor), A. Bentley, P. Hions and Ward Barraclough.

he led to what was described as the most successful period in the band's history during his eighteen months as its leader. He was then elected to the position of band conductor, and he was soon to be in demand by many other local bands in the Halifax district, as his reputation as a skilful band trainer grew. During this period he was combining his talents as a solo cornet player at contests and concert engagements with many of the local bands, including King Cross, Lee Mount, Sowerby Bridge and the Friendly Band. He soon gained the reputation as a player who 'gave his all'.

Local orchestral societies were regularly seeking his services as well, but at this time he suffered a setback when he became seriously ill, and for a time had to stop all his musical activities. However, he did eventually join another band as the principal solo cornet: the 1st V.B. Duke of Wellington's West Riding Regimental Band (which in later years became the 4th Battalion Territorials). He stayed with the 'Dukes' for the next three years, during which time, as a volunteer bandsman, he was promoted to deputy bandmaster and band sergeant. His unassuming manner and ability as a trainer was appreciated, and he was respected by everyone.

He was asked on a number of occasions to conduct the Brighouse and Rastrick Temperance Band, and after leaving the 'Dukes' was offered the position on a full-time basis. During his time at Brighouse he and the band was very successful in the contest field, and he was rightly very proud that its success had been achieved without the help of a professional conductor (a practice that most of the bigger bands adopted).

Having left Brighouse, he accepted the position of bandmaster at the famous King Cross (Halifax) Band, a band that had the legendary William Rimmer as its professional musical director. This was a very prestigious appointment for Arthur. It is said that William Rimmer himself complimented him on the rapid progress the band was making. The band entered the prestigious Crystal Palace national band contest, which was to be held in September 1909. However, two weeks before the big day William Rimmer informed the band committee that, owing to insufficient dates available for him to rehearse the band, he wished to be relieved from his engagement for this contest. The band members were extremely disappointed, but as a show of confidence in their own bandmaster decided to go to the contest without the services of a professional conductor, and ask Mr Pearce to take the band. The band spent

Black Dyke Mills Band. From left to right (starting at the top): Geoffrey Whitham, Wally Shaw, Gordon Sutcliffe, the band bus driver, Ivor Judson, Arthur Oldfield, Donald Woodhead, Bernard Burns, Leslie Langforde, Ewart Armitage, Frank Hiley, Billie Land, Harry Nelson, Charlie Emmott, George Mortimer, Percy Hughes, Haydn Robinson, Jo Wood, Denzil Stephens, Alan Bentley, Owen Bottomley, Harry Beckwith, Ernest Keaton, AOP, Albert Frost, Wilf Kershaw, and, on the side, Alwyn Pinches and Albert Brown.

hours putting the final touches to what was a difficult piece in its day (Charles Godfrey's arrangement of Wagner's *The Flying Dutchman*). In the end, the Shaw Band came first – under the baton of none other than William Rimmer – and the King Cross (Halifax) Band came sixth. The programme shows the band had been conducted by William Rimmer, however, we now know that the band was conducted by Arthur.

Another momentous occasion for the band and its bandmaster was in the summer of 1911 when Arthur O. Pearce had the distinction of conducting the band in the presence of King George V at Buckingham Palace, on the eve of the King's coronation. (He was considered to be both the bandmaster and the conductor, following the band's decision not to engage a professional conductor for the 1911 season.)

Arthur maintained that the effort and dedication displayed at a concert should be the same as at a contest, a philosophy that was to later be reflected at the Black Dyke Mills Band throughout his thirty-seven years as its bandmaster. The King Cross Band had undoubtedly prospered under his direction. His reputation as a band trainer placed him in constant demand by other bands, both to perform as a guest conductor and with tempting offers to take over permanently.

On 1 January 1912 he finally agreed to become the bandmaster of the Black Dyke Mills Band, a position he was to hold until his retirement on 31 December 1948. His first public engagement with the band was at the Victoria Hall in Halifax, where a new feature of the band was introduced at this, and at all future concerts: as he walked on stage the band members would spring to attention, acknowledging the audience and Mr Pearce.

The period from 1912 through to 1928 were the great days of the legendary St Hilda's Colliery Band, who were the Champion Band of Great Britain in 1912, 1920, 1921, 1924 and 1926. It is generally accepted that if it were not for the war years, when the contest was suspended, St Hilda's would have been a difficult band to beat. However, Black Dyke was rarely out of the top six at this time, and 1928 was the band's turning point: on Saturday 29 September the band lined up against fourteen other bands to take on Gustav Holst's *A Moorside Suite*. Playing off No. 4 and under the baton of its professional conductor, William Halliwell, the band had to wait until after the evening massed-band concert and a performance of *Alpine Echoes* by guest soloist Jack Mackintosh to find out it had won.

Above: *It was celebration time at Queensbury when Black Dyke Mills Band was awarded the title of National Brass Band Champions of Great Britain for 1947. Little did the members know then that this was the first of a hat-trick of wins with Harry Mortimer. The man lying on the floor is Hayden Robinson, the band's solo trombone player.*

Left: *With Joe Wood in 1950, looking through some of the many gifts he received on his retirement. Joe had the unenviable task of stepping into Arthur O. Pearce's shoes following his retirement.*

I was thirteen years old when I played with the Queensbury Schools Band. I then joined the Black Dyke Mills Junior Band. When I left school I went to work at John Foster's Black Dyke Mills in the mechanic's department. This was the first time I came in contact with Arthur O. Pearce. He was a mechanic in the same department, although he worked in a different section, and we were barely on nodding terms, me being the youngest lad in the department. He always referred to himself as the 'Foreman Mechanic and Bandmaster', even though he was not really in charge of anyone.

In those days the conductor did everything including all the band secretarial work, which he did using the bed of his lathe as his desk. He was not someone you could have a joke with: he was always a serious man, and I would often see him turning his waxed moustache.

Smith Patchett was the second baritone player in 1946 and had decided to retire. I was invited by A.O.P. to audition with the senior band. The area test piece in 1946 was John Ireland's *Downland Suite*. I didn't play at that contest nor did the band qualify for the National Finals in London. I joined the band after that disappointment and recall there was an inquest back at the bandroom afterwards as to why the band had not qualified. A.O.P. suggested that they get a second opinion; the man who came was Harry Mortimer, someone else who I had never met before.

As a young member of the band you were never allowed to call him by his first name: it was always 'Mr Pearce'. Only a select few of the most senior players had that privilege.
John Slinger, baritone player at Black Mills Band from 1946 to 1989

Arthur Pearce was a strict disciplinarian but a very fair man; everybody in the band was treated as equal – his only aim was always for the good of his band. In 1947 I was a young boy working in the Spinning Office at John Foster & Sons when a call came on the internal phone for me to go and see Mr Pearce at his place of work.

On my arrival he said, 'Last night I sacked the second baritone player – not for his playing but because we wouldn't help with the kit. I am offering you the job on a month's trial.' Of course I accepted, but he made me ring my father for his permission; of course he gave it, and I was told to pick up the baritone after work at the bandroom – he went on to say that should I slip up either playing or in my behaviour I too would be out.

At my first rehearsal with the band I wanted to do everything right – I was tapping my foot for the timing, and he yelled at me 'keep it still!' and scared me to death. We young ones had to be at the bandroom at 7 p.m. on Monday and Thursday evenings to help with putting the music out for the rehearsal. He would then tell us the history of the band until everyone else arrived and the rehearsal started at 7.30 p.m., exactly – not a minute before, not a minute after. He'd finish at 9.30 p.m., on the dot.

In the October of that year the band won the National Championships for the first of a hat-trick of wins. Harry Mortimer conducted the band at the Royal Albert Hall, although the programme notes indicated A.O. Pearce as conductor. It was after the 1948 win that Mr Pearce retired.

I played at Arthur Pearce's retirement concert, a concert that Brighouse and Rastrick also took part in, as he was one of their former cornet players, in his younger days. A lasting memory from that concert was when Willie Lang and Harry Mortimer played the cornet duet *Ida and Dot* together, with both bands being conducted by Fred Mortimer.

I am of the opinion that Arthur O. Pearce has been the best bandmaster throughout the brass band movement.

Geoffrey Whitham – Black Dyke Mills Band principal euphonium and conductor

From being a thirteen-year-old bugle player with a Scout Band and taking cornet lessons at half a crown a time from Mr Tom Atkinson (who was head of brass music for the Bradford Education Authority), it was a great surprise to me to be approached by a distinguished gentleman after I had played at a slow melody contest in Bradford early in 1945 when I was seventeen years old.

He asked me if I would like to join the Black Dyke Mills Band on repiano cornet and be featured as a boy soloist because Owen Bottomley, the band's principal cornet, was finding the going rather tough. Of course I said 'Yes,' and with Bernard Burn's, the band's soprano cornet player's expert tuition, I was featured at the band's concerts and during a BBC broadcast from Leeds. What amazed me was that I was expected to play the triple-tonguing cornet solo *Jenny Wren*, which included a sprinkling of top Cs, when Mr Pearce had only heard me play a slow melody once.

All went well and I am grateful for the help and guidance that the band members gave me. That wondrous introduction to the band gave me the confidence to accept the position of principal cornet for three years in the 1950s until the arrival of Maurice Murphy, who I was privileged to sit next to.

David Pratt, member of Black Dyke Mills Band as the repiano cornet player (1945/46), principal cornet player (1953-1956), and assistant principal cornet player to Maurice Murphy and James Shepherd (from 1956 to his retirement in 1970)

In 1933 Arthur celebrated twenty-one years as Black Dyke's bandmaster. During that time, the band had won over £16,000 in prize money, in addition to winning twenty-nine challenge trophies, fourteen instruments, thirty-nine gold medals and thirty-five silver medals. The band was placed first on eighteen occasions, second on nineteen occasions, third on five occasions and fourth on five occasions. It also won the World Championship once, came second four times, won the £1,500 Gold Shield at Glasgow two years in succession (when each player was also awarded a gold medal), and took the £250 challenge bowl at Newcastle twice in succession. At Firhill, Glasgow in 1931, the band won the International Contest Challenge Cup and £100 prize money. The band was also carrying out an equally unprecedented number of prestigious concerts the length and breadth of the country (estimated to have been between 100 and 150 annually). In the summer of 1933 Arthur led the band on a 4,000-mile tour; this had only been beaten in 1906, when the band travelled 15,000 miles and gave over 200 performances on its five-month American and Canadian tour. On that memorable trip, one concert in Montreal was performed in front of over 40,000 people; comparisons between Black Dyke and the great John Philip Sousa were talked of.

In January 1949, at the age of seventy-seven, Arthur lead his beloved Black Dyke for the last time. He had decided it was time to retire, and the Victoria Hall at Halifax seemed the most appropriate venue for his final performance as it was here where it all started thirty-seven years earlier.

During the war years he had also been the conductor of the Halifax Special Constabulary Band, and he led the band at over 178 free concerts and also at many broadcasts. However, between 1925 and 1948 he led Black Dyke through a total of 205 broadcasts for the BBC alone.

The Iles Medal is awarded by the Worshipful Company of Musicians for significant contributions to the brass band movement. It seemed fitting that Arthur O. Pearce was chosen to be the first recipient of the medal, and on the 11 January 1948 he was presented with the medal at the Temperance Hall in Huddersfield during one of the band's broadcasts.

On Saturday, 17 January 1951, aged seventy-nine years, Arthur O. Pearce died – during his thirty-seven years with Black Dyke he had conducted the band before some of the country's leading musicians, including Sir Edward Elgar, Sir Granville Bantock and Joseph Holbrooke, to name just three. On his death certificate, dated 13 January 1951, his occupation is shown as 'textile mill maintenance engineer (retired) and the Bandmaster of Black Dyke Mills Band'.

My first memory of Mr Arthur O. Pearce was the meeting in the bandroom one day in 1945 prior to being accepted into the Black Dyke Mills Band. He appeared to me then as being a severe-looking gentleman wearing pince-nez and sporting a waxed moustache. His eyes were piercing, and there was a stern look on his face.

He was a strict disciplinarian, insisting on good time-keeping. No one dared to be late for rehearsal or engagements. I remember one day the coach setting off from Queensbury for the BBC Studio in Leeds without one member of the band. When I asked a senior player what would happen, I was told the player had to make his own way to the studio in time for the recording, or lose his place in the band!

There was a softer side to Mr Pearce, however. I was keen on writing music even as a young teenager, and I asked A.O. for permission to try out a euphonium solo with the band. He not only gave me this permission, but included it in a program broadcast by BBC Leeds.

Ladies were not allowed on the band coach, so I had doubts about asking A.O. for permission to take my fiancée, Glenys, to a BBC recording as a birthday treat. Imagine my surprise when he agreed! To counter that, when I later married Glenys in 1950 on a sunny Saturday, I was not allowed to go on my honeymoon until I had played with the band in Manningham Park, Bradford on the Sunday, in both the afternoon and evening performances.

Denzil Stephens, solo euphonium player and member of Black Dyke Mills Band, 1945-1950

PETER WADSWORTH
'Always the dedicated bandsman'

My first contest dates back to about 1960, at a venue that was hardly the most prestigious of concert halls. However, the Sowerby Bridge swimming baths – or Princess Ballroom, as it became in the winter after the pool had been boarded over – was then the venue for the Halifax and District Band Association's annual winter contest.

I was one of the younger members of the Clifton and Lightcliffe Band, in fact the principal third cornet. Sounds impressive, but then again there was only me. I cannot remember what test piece we played but there are two things that I do have a vivid memories of from that occasion: firstly, we didn't win; and secondly, watching the Lindley Band of Huddersfield. The musical director, Peter Wadsworth, was dressed, as he always was in those days, in his distinctive black police inspector's uniform. On that day the band played Percy Fletcher's famous 1913 test piece *Labour and Love*, and was easily the best band on show.

Lindley Band. Standing at the back in uniform is one of the parent supporters of the band. From left to right, back row: Peter Sheard, Ralph Wadsworth, Kenneth Thorpe, ? Telford, Douglas Telford. Middle row: -?-, Jack Botterill (who went on to be a member of the Squadronaires); Arnold ?, Maurice Alport, Frank Matheson (who was the Bass Trombone player at the London Symphony Orchestra for thirty years), Kenneth Sarsby (bass trombone player at B&R Band), Maurice Wadsworth (second euphonium for B&R Band). Front row: Brian Rawlinson, Geoffrey York, Roy Smith, Peter Wadsworth, Tim Wadsworth, Herbert Luty, Frank Berry (the principal trombone for Black Dyke Mills Band), Keith Barron (or 'Steamboat', as he was known in the band).

This band's story begins with Peter's father, Tim, who was his greatest musical influence. Tim came from a musical family: his nephew Maurice played second euphonium to Fred Spencer at Brighouse and Rastrick, and his eldest brother Harry was a cornet player. Going back further still, his grandfather, John Beaumont, conducted the Holmfirth Rifle Band.

By the time Peter was born in February 1922 the family was living in the Manchester district of Whalley Range, but six months later his parents moved the family to Huddersfield. In 1935, Tim was invited to become the conductor at Lindley Band, which he accepted. It was a difficult task as many of the older and more experienced players had become involved in the war effort, which left the band comprising mainly of enthusiastic youngsters.

One of the earliest documented references to the Lindley Band is in the late 1830s in the local parish register, which records that a group of players from the village of Lindley organised to play at a Sunday service at St Stephens. Lindley Brass Band is also recorded in the minutes of the Lindley Zion School as engaged to perform for their Whitsuntide parade in 1835. The school minutes record that a fee was paid plus beer for band members. One can only speculate what may have happened, as the following year it was minuted that milk was to be provided for the younger members of the band!

At the age of seven Peter was already a chorister at his local church. This, along with piano lessons given by the church organist and choirmaster, William Greenwood, was his childhood introduction to what was to become almost a lifetime in music. At fourteen, he tried the cornet and then the soprano cornet, but then he finally moved on to what he considered to be his instrument, the euphonium. In 1936 he joined his dad as the new euphonium player at Lindley Band.

In the early post-war period the band had some early success on the contest platform. In 1947, at the Yorkshire third section area contest, the band was awarded second place. Then, in 1948, Peter took on the new role as musical director at Lindley. He soon followed in his dad's footsteps when the band was awarded third place at the Yorkshire second section area contest. Over the next twenty-five years Peter was to lead the band through a period of unprecedented success.

One of Peter's earliest contest memories as the new conductor goes back to the 1951 Spring Festival, Grand Shield at Belle Vue in Manchester. The band was drawn fairly late on, but as the time to play drew nearer it soon became apparent that the soprano cornet and one of the solo cornet players were cutting it a bit fine from a trip into Manchester. With only minutes to go, and both of the players still missing, decisions had to be taken. Peter quickly re-scored the two parts for other players to cover and the band took to the stage with both players missing.

What the adjudicator's remarks made of it has long since been forgotten, but Peter, with a certain amount of pride, remembers the band was placed first ahead of rivals Askern Colliery and Crossley Carpets Band. Just what was said to the two missing players when they did finally turn up is probably unprintable.

From a band initially consisting of youngsters the band was now beginning to attract older and more experienced players. Looking through the band's results, pride of place for Peter were the two occasions when he led the band to a higher placement than the more famous Black Dyke Mills Band at Belle Vue on consecutive years.

The band's performances went from strength to strength, so much so that during the 1960s the band was able to employ the services of Leonard Lamb (musical director of the Fairey Band) as the band's professional conductor for the prestige contests. In the late 1960s and early '70s the band also employed the professional services of Ernest Woodhouse and Edmund Hoole. In 1975 Peter stepped down after forty years at Lindley, as both a player and conductor – the time had come for someone else to take over and build on the foundation he had out in place.

Peter Wadsworth, fourth row from the back with his distinctive black hair, and his very successful Lindly band during the early 1970s.

I was about twelve years old, so it would be about 1940, and I was playing around an old brick building in Lindley called The Old Bandroom with my friend Jack Botterill when an old man (he seemed old to a twelve year old) came out and asked what we were doing. Knowing it was the bandroom, I cheekily said 'We've come to join the band', which wasn't really true. That was the beginning of my musical career and when I first met Peter Wadsworth.

As a player we looked up to Peter as the solo euphonium. Having graduated from the Junior Band I became as member of the Lindley Brass Band after the war. We played concerts in Greenhead Park and marched around the streets at galas and so called 'Rants'. Then there were the contests at Belle Vue – these were big days. Peter was very committed to the band and to his father, the conductor. My musical knowledge in those days was very limited but I do remember at Belle Vue one particular year Peter being in tears because he had fluffed a solo in the test piece *Labour and Love* we were playing.

As kids in the band Peter always called me 'Mathy', something I challenged him about: he said it was a term of affection, and of course I accepted that, but always wished he would call me Frank ... Many years later I met Peter again. It was at the Holmfirth contest, and Peter was conducting Scapegoat Hill Band during the mid-1980s ... [and] even after all those years, he still called me Mathy.

Peter was always a dedicated bandsman and always did his utmost to get the best out of his band.

Frank Mathison, bass trombone with the London Symphony Orchestra for thirty years

Hepworth Band in 1981. From left to right, back row: S. Robinson; S. Pollitt and S. Lindley. Third row: A. Holmes, B. Sykes, J. Holmes, M. Walker, S. Thewlis, H. Sykes, K. Haigh, J. Young, C. Slater and B. Brook. Second row: H. Taylor, N. Kaye, J. Hellawell, A. Mitchell, M. Golden, R. Holmes, G. Goldthorpe, M. England and Peter Wadsworth. Front row: I. Mellor, D. Roebuck, Jeffrey Turner, R. Sutton, G. Oldroyd, H. Hill, M. Drew, D. Tinker and Mrs R. Golden.

After a short spell at Walkden Band in Lancashire he was invited to be the new conductor at Slaithwaite Band. In his first contest the band was awarded third place at the Belle Vue, Grand Shield Contest in 1976. Two years later he was on the move again, but only the short trip to near-neighbours Hepworth Band.

After a successful four-year period at Hepworth he moved on to what was to become his last band, when in 1984 he conducted another Huddersfield area band at Scapegoat Hill, a position he held for three years. In 1986 he decided it was time to call it a day.

Since his tenure at Scapegoat Hill came to an end Peter had no further active involvement with brass bands. Peter died in March 2008 aged 86.

EDDIE WILLIAMS

'Remembered for his outstanding musical ability and integrity'

I have vivid memories of watching the championship section bands at the Royal Albert Hall during the 1960s, when, like all young cornet-playing teenagers at that time, I knew all the top bands and the big-name players because they were all household names. However, there was one band I have to confess which I knew nothing about back in those days. This was probably due to the fact it was based over 350 miles from my home at Lightcliffe. That band was St Dennis of Cornwall, but the one thing that I do remember was the name on the programme of the conductor: E. Williams. I am now pleased after all these years to have the opportunity of looking back on a man who gave so much to the brass band movement in his native county of Cornwall, and in particular to the St Dennis Band.

The band is believed to have been started during Queen Victoria's pre-coronation celebrations of 1836. In 1928 the band really did well when it was awarded first place and crowned Grand Shield (second section) champions at the Crystal Palace, and again in 1938 at the Alexandra Palace after the Crystal Palace had burnt down two years earlier.

The band is probably the only West of England band to play before royalty, and that was in the presence of the Prince of Wales before the Second World War, when the band had a hat-trick of wins in the West of England Brass Band Championships. The band members on that momentous occasion were each presented with a set of special commemorative medals by the prince.

Under the baton of Charles H. Baker, the 1930s proved to be a good time for the band, competing in the Crystal Palace Championship section each year from 1929 to 1932. The band's early conductors included: W.H. Juleff (1909-1923), R.W. Davidson (1923-1924), Edwin Calverley (1924-1925 from Bacup) and Charles H. Baker, (1926-1949 from Rushden).

In 1951, along with Camborne Band under the baton of Fred Roberts and St Dennis conducted by William (Bill) D. Lawton, (the former front row cornet player from Foden's Motor Works Band), both bands competed in the championship section at the Royal Albert Hall. Whilst neither band was in the prizes this was the start of another good time for St Dennis Band.

Throughout the 1950s the band was able to attract some of the bigger-named conductors at the time, including John Harrison and George Thompson. In 1958 the band appointed Edwin John Williams (junior) as the musical director, and for the next twenty-five years he guided the band through its most successful period.

Edwin (Eddie) John Williams was born in Bugle in Cornwall and was the only son of Edwin and Martha Williams. He was part of a large musical family. His father was a euphonium

With cornet in hand, young Eddie stands alongside his father, Edwin John Williams, in his conductor's frock coat.

player and conductor of brass bands and mixed choirs, as well as being a local composer and music arranger. His mother was a fine contralto singer and also played the baritone. She had the distinction of being the first female to play in the celebrated bugle brass band contest. Many of Eddie's uncles were bandsmen as well, playing with local bands in Wales. Most of his aunts were either singers or played brass instruments.

Eddie's musical career started on the cornet in the Caharrack and St Day Band, a few miles from Redruth; his father was the conductor. But Eddie was destined for a bright future in the world of brass bands and was soon on the move. His first taste of playing at a higher level of band was when he moved to Camborne Town Band, not as a cornet player but as the band's new solo horn player.

In 1941 Eddie successfully auditioned for a vacancy at Brighouse and Rastrick and was there until January 1946, leaving to join the forces. He was hoping to continue his playing during his army service but the only way he could was to change instruments to the French horn. He refused. As soon as he left the army he resumed his band career by accepting the position of solo horn at Camborne, under the baton of Fred Roberts, the ex-Brighouse and Rastrick principal cornet player.

In 1953 he was given the opportunity of auditioning for Fairey Aviation Works Band at Stockport, after Harry Farrington emigrated to New Zealand. His audition was to play in a concert at Bolton Town Hall, on what was a miserable January night in 1954. Unfamiliar with this part of the world, Eddie was met at the railway station in Manchester by Kenneth Dennison. Eddie and Kenneth boarded the Fairey's coach to Bolton, and during the journey he was kitted out with a uniform. Kenneth remembers that Eddie's performance at the concert was excellent. It was of course pure sight reading, and included the awkward solo in the *Poet and Peasant* overture. Eddie also did a stand-up solo from a manuscript he had brought with him. This was real edge-of-the-seat playing for everyone, because Fairey's had not seen his solo *The Spinning Wheel* either.

In 1954 the championship section test piece was Frank Wright's arrangement of Jack Beaver's (1900-1963) *Sovereign Heritage*, which has a particularly difficult quartet cadenza. Part of the band's preparation included Norman Ashcroft (cornet), Harry Cheshire (euphonium), Kenneth Dennison (trombone) and Eddie (on horn) meeting at Fairey's bandroom every morning to go through the cadenza and play it through at least three times. On Saturday 16 October, playing off No. 6, Harry Mortimer brought his baton down and fifteen minutes later it was all over: a hat-trick of wins for H.M. (1952 with Fairey's; 1953 with Foden's.)

At the evening concert nine massed bands took part and the test piece was included. This piece had not been rehearsed for the concert with so many on the stage, and when it came time for the cadenza which should have been played by thirty-six players, the conductor Frank Wright simply put down his baton down and looked at his finger nails. Taking into account the spread across the stage taken up by the 225 players, the various sections were equally well spread apart. For the first note of the cadenza only one player came in, and that was Harry

Cheshire on euphonium, followed by one cornet (Norman Ashcroft), one horn (Eddie) and, finally recognising his three colleagues, Kenneth Dennison as the solitary trombone player. Kenneth recalls, 'It worked like a dream, and on the recording it sounds as if we were all very close together, so our preparation did pay off.'

During Eddie's time at Fairey's the view was that he did a first-class job and he would probably have stayed but for the strong pull of his native Cornwall, which was to finally draw him back to St Dennis.

In 1958 Eddie, his wife Lorna, and their young daughter Alison moved back to Cornwall, and he was

St Dennis Youth Band (Eddie Williams is centre front row), winners of the 1976 West of England Regional Qualifying Finals of the Butlin's Youth Brass Band Championships.

appointed the conductor of St Dennis Band. For the next twenty-five years he guided the band to its most successful period, and few would doubt that they became the best band in the West of England. Under Eddie's direction the band qualified for the top section of the National Finals no less than fifteen times, gaining sixth place in 1978 playing the Sir Arthur Bliss test piece *Checkmate*. The band also competed at the British Open at Belle Vue on three occasions in the 1960s. In Cornwall the band won the famous West of England Bandsmen's Festival (Bugle) The Royal Trophy on seventeen occasions during Eddie's reign at the band. In addition, in 1962 Eddie formed the junior band at St Dennis's and also conducted the Cornwall Youth Band.

Throughout his musical career he was always supported by his family. Lorna ensured that Eddie was always the smartest member of the band. She was always in the audience to listen to the band both at contests as well as concerts, and was always the supportive hostess when Eddie suddenly arrived home after an evening rehearsal with members of a visiting band or a guest soloist. Alison followed in her father's footsteps, but after a period as a cornet player she moved on to the horn, and played in both the junior and senior bands at St Dennis.

Through his musical career Eddie made many lasting friendships: Tommy Rouse, who played baritone at Camborne Band, was best man at his wedding; Emlyn Bryant, soprano and Ken Dennison were both friends and colleagues at Fairey's. As a young brass player his greatest influence was from his father, but in later life he thought very highly of both Eric Ball and Harry Mortimer. His life's ambition as a musician was to be the best, and one day play with a top-class band, and he certainly achieved that ambition.

After every contest, win or lose, he would analyze not only the band's performance but his own as well – had he prepared the band correctly? Then he moved onto the next performance, always learning from the last one. Eddie was not just a brass musician and brass band conductor either, his musical activities went beyond that. His father had both started and conducted the Lanner Home Guard Choir, and when his father died Eddie took over that role. He also went on to conduct the Redruth Ladies' Choir.

Eddie will obviously be remembered for his work and success with St Dennis Band, and for his services to brass bands he was awarded the Iles Medal in 1981. His work with youth bands earned him the Bard of the Cornish Gorseth, and he was the only man ever to receive the Prince of Wales medal at the Bugle contest on six occasions.

The 1956 Champion Quartet of Great Britain from Fairey Aviation Works Band. Left to right: Brian Mather, Ian Gladstone, Leonard Lamb (who joined as a tutti cornet player in 1938), George Miller and Eddie Williams.

Eddie was always in demand to help and train the lower section bands, particularly before a contest. Eddie came from an era of earning little more than travelling expenses, and the joy of helping others; that was enough for him. With his experience in Fairey's quartet this was a particular area of banding he enjoyed, and was always on hand to help out in any way he could.

Lorna is proud to look back on how many of Eddie's pupils went on to conduct bands of their own and play in other bands at the highest level. One cornet player even went on to play with the Royal Ballet in London.

Sadly Eddie died in 1983, and as well as being a great loss to his family, his passing saw the fortunes of the St Dennis Band go into a decline. Throughout the 1990s the band struggled, and while we often read about bands who would rather close down than start again in the fourth section, no one was throwing the towel in at St Dennis Band.

Brian Minear, who conducted the present St Dennis Band until quite recently, has fond memories of his old friend 'E.J.', as his close friends always called him. Brian has been associated with St Dennis since he was first invited to join almost fifty years ago, from his position as principal cornet at the Cornwall Youth Brass Band. During his association with the band he was not only the band's principal cornet player but also the solo euphonium and solo horn (not at the same time, he is quick to point out!), and he played with the band throughout the Eddie Williams era. During the 1980s, owing to the pressure of work, Brian left St Dennis Band but maintained his contact with banding in the South West.

No sooner had Brian taken early retirement in 2001 than he successfully auditioned to be the musical director of St Dennis Band. Through Brian's inspiration (and, no doubt, his long association playing under 'E.J.'), and experience, he successfully took the band from the depths of the fourth section to a challenging position in 2009. Recently Brian decided it was time to pass the reins on to someone else to give the band fresh impetus and take it onward and upward.

Brian stills talks fondly of his old friend and says that Eddie's legacy remains at St Dennis Band, and he will always be remembered and respected for his many qualities and his outstanding musical ability and integrity.

5

MUSICAL STEPPING STONES

Phillip Hunt learnt the tenor horn with The Torpoint Town Band, but gave up playing and moved into administration, becoming involved with The South West Brass Band Association as Treasurer, Secretary and Chairman over a period of nearly thirty years. At the same time he became founding Secretary of The Council of West England Brass Bands Associations, which is responsible for the organisation of The West of England Brass Band Championships. It is also responsible for the application of The National Rules and Gradings in the region and through this he served for ten years on The National Contesting Council, the overall national ruling body at the time of The Brass Band Movement.

Phillip started broadcasting brass band programmes on BBC Radio Devon when the station started in 1983. His current programme, Sounds of Brass, first went on the air in September 1985, and has been broadcast every week ever since. The 1,000th programme went out on 26 February 2006 and it is now in its twenty-fourth year. It was extended to BBC Cornwall in 1994 and from January 2004 to seven other BBC local radio stations in the West of England, making a total of nine, inlcuding Jersey and Guernsey.

GEORGE SWIFT

'Introduced to professional music ... through brass bands'

In recent years I have met a number of people whose introduction to professional music came through being involved in brass bands. An example of this is the late George Swift, who started in brass bands and went on to make a full-time career out of music.

George was born in South Shields in the North of England in 1911. He started playing the cornet at the age of ten with the Bolden Colliery Band. At the age of fifteen, George joined the famous St Hilda's Colliery Band, as a boy cornetist, and was soon playing all the popular solos of the day.

In 1930 he joined the professional world of dance bands and went on tour in Germany and Switzerland. In 1934 he joined a German dance band and later that year he received a telephone call from band leader Jack Hylton in London asking him to join his orchestra. During the Second World War George was playing with the band of the Irish Guards and performing for troops in England, North Africa and Italy. After the war he was freelancing around the London theatres and with society dance bands. He was in great demand during the late 1940s. At the beginning of the war he had been invited to play in the Mantovani Orchestra. This was during his service with the Irish Guards, and when he was playing he used to wear his khaki under his evening dress so that he could make a quick change into uniform if the Military Police turned up.

He joined Mantovani on a regular basis in around 1960, but still found time to be involved in session work and with the Scottish Variety Orchestra. However, in 1965, the Swift family left their home in Stanmore, Middlesex and settled in Marbella. On 13 April 1985, having returned to England, George Swift died at the age of seventy-four, in a nursing home in Bexhill on the south coast of England.

NIGEL CARTER

'It was those early days that gave me my musical start'

Nigel with trumpet in full flow. The saxophonist (to the left) is thought to be Ronnie Scott, he of the famous Ronnie Scott's Jazz Club in London.

As the dark clouds of war arrived in 1939, Eric and Nellie Carter were anxious to get their young family out of Salford. They had three children: Roy, Margaret and Nigel, who was barely a year old when the family moved to the comparative safety of Peak Dale near Buxton in Derbyshire.

Nigel's introduction to music came through his older brother Roy. Even though their father was a pianist and liked to sing, Nigel says it wasn't really a musical family. He was introduced to the world of brass instruments through the Peak Dale Band. His earliest memory of the band goes back to about 1944: he can recall the bandmaster, Reg Hallam, who was also a cornet player, and Len Hoyle, who was a tuba player and someone who very meticulously greased all the valves and slides of the band's instruments. It was Len Hoyle who promised to give Nigel his first old Higham's cornet, and Nigel would swing on his garden gate as a constant reminder until he kept his promise. One of Nigel's oldest friends, David Garner, is still associated with Peak Dale Band.

These were difficult times for band funding, and Nigel recalls paying a shilling in order to join the band. The band room in those days was an old church that had been bought from a neighbouring village fifteen miles away some years earlier. It was dismantled very carefully and then transported by a team of men on the back of a horse and cart. Back in the days when we had 'proper' winters, the snow was so deep that one year the only way into the band room was to dig a tunnel underneath.

Nigel's first cornet teacher was Reg Hallam; his older brother Roy took over, and then Jack Fletcher. It was Reg who taught Nigel the basics of general banding and the art of slow melody playing. His brother Roy found and gave him an old Rudy Muck 17C short cornet mouthpiece, which had been made in New York, something Nigel gladly accepted. This enabled him to play those 'step ladder notes', and more importantly to play them quietly, and brought about his first change of instrument, from cornet to soprano. For many years later he used that same mouthpiece on his trumpet, but with the help of an added extension adapter. From as early as eight years old, Nigel had two musical directions, brass bands and traditional jazz.

Another of Nigel's early influences was his teacher Jack Fletcher, who used to play at Creswell Colliery Band. He was very kind and left such an impression that Nigel named his own son John Fletcher Carter after him. It was Jack who taught Nigel to play Bb cornet parts on the Eb soprano. This was to lead him into playing at variety and concert dates and in later years playing alongside jazz legend Humphrey Lyttleton. He was soon invited to be a jazz soloist at the Royal Albert Hall. When he was fifteen or sixteen he was approached by Frank

Peak Dale Band in around 1948, winners of the march class at Tideswell band festival, and runners-up in the Challenge Cup Competition (won by Burslem Co-op Prize Band). Nigel can be seen kneeling in the front row on the left, next to the double Bb bass.

Moss, who in the early 1950s was the conductor at the newly formed Ferodo Works Band, to join the band on soprano. The solo cornet player at Ferodo at that time was Bernard Bygraves. Nigel was very impressed with the band at his first rehearsal and recalls the band membership in those early days was made up of local players who had come from many of the surrounding bands including Chapel-en-le-Frith, Dove Holes and Buxton.

He only stayed at Ferodo for a short while because the opportunities of going freelance in the local dance band scene were drawing him away. In 1955, then aged seventeen, he was invited back but this time on Bb cornet. It was during his second spell at Ferodo that he had the opportunity of seeing and hearing one of the all-time great cornet players in action: Willie Lang. Nigel can still remember his sound, which he describes as being very focused, and he played the cornet like a violin, with beautiful phrasing and an innate sense of what is fine and true.

Not long after Nigel had gone back to Ferodo, Willie Lang left to join the Halle Orchestra. The Ferodo band met up with Willie for at least one performance when the whole band was asked by Sir John Barbirolli to enhance their brass section for a performance of the *1812 Overture*.

By now the band's ambitions were moving quickly ahead which saw the appointment of George Hespe as the musical director. Nigel describes George Hespe as being progressive in his programme choice; he even on occasions allowed him to play stand up solo jazz style pieces.

Another player Nigel recalls was the trombone player Ernie Appleyard, a businessman from Yorkshire whose speciality solo was *Love's Enchantment*. George Hespe, Ernie Appleyard, Willie Lang and Nigel all enjoyed the flexibility of being able to take on freelance work. However, the day of reckoning came when he was sent for by the works' public-relations management. They asked if he would take a full-time job at the works, and they gave him a job amidst the fumes in the processing plant. This was too much for any young musician. He went on to try an engineering course, but his heart was not in it. However, he had just bought a BSA Bantam Major motorcycle, and needed to pay for it somehow! So after sticking it out for eighteen months and having paid for his motorcycle, off came the overalls and he said goodbye to a life in engineering. Music was his calling, and would be for the rest of his working life.

Playing at the Isle of Man was something the members of Ferodo Band looked forward to. Here the band takes a break after playing in the summer sun.

Ferodo Works Band, British Open Champions, with musical director George W. Hespe, ARCM, LRAM, in 1955. From left to right, back row: Walter Pearson, Matthew Marshall, William (Bill) Skelton, William Fletcher, Ernest Appleyard, Campbell Holmes, Derek Roebuck. Middle row: Graham White, Eric Bland, Nigel Carter, Cliff Lack, Keith Caldwell, Les Holden, William Morley, Jack Allcock, Alf Garlick, Frank Slater. Front row: Fred Evans, Ray English, Marcus Cutts, Donald Marshall, Ronald Harrison, Jimmy Mycock, William Bagguley and Solomon Clayton.

Nigel's tuition fee in those days was *2s 6d*, but Jack always refunded him *6d* explaining, 'Two bob fo't master and a tanner fo't lad', a phrase that is still with Nigel today and one he often uses after teaching his granddaughter Rachel to play the violin. Having started playing the old Higham's cornet at seven, within two years he had also started to play the trumpet.

Ferodo's had a change of heart and let him stay on in the band until he was called up for his National Service, serving for two years in the Royal Signals Band. (Going to the Royal Signals was the suggestion of George Hespe.) After his initial training he spent the next two years playing marches for the soldiers' passing-out parades, fanfares for ceremonial occasions and of course Big Band music. There were cathedral organists, singers, string players; in fact there was every kind of musician you could think of, as well as artists, poets and a ballet dancer. Between 1957 and 1959 the Royal Signals Band had over 100 members.

After he was demobbed Nigel played with a number of dance bands, and in 1962 he even went to play around Scotland for a short while. Once he was invited to join the Ken Mackintosh Band, and he was often invited to play in other bands, such as Harry Leader and Syd Dean, who were all prolific broadcasting bands. His days in the world of brass bands had come to an end.

He then moved on to be a studio player (which meant his playing was devoted exclusively to television, musical jingles and the recording studio). After the heady days and life as a freelance player, in 1972 he joined the BBC Radio Orchestra/Radio Big Band, and he is still there, having been leader and first trumpet for well over thirty years. Today he plays alongside another familiar name from the world of brass bands, Brian Rankine, who played with Kinneil Colliery Band during the 1960s.

His early musical influences were the brass band greats of the time, CWS (Manchester) Band, Black Dyke Mills Band and of course the Ferodo Works Band. Once he moved into the world of jazz his musical influences changed to include such names as King Oliver, Kid Ory and of course Louis Armstrong. As all musicians know, your own personal musical influences are constantly evolving, and in Nigel's case they now also include Stan Kenton, Billy May, Duke Ellington and Count Basie. He now enjoys classical music equally as much but his number one musical hero is the international trumpet player Maurice André.

There have been a few ups and downs in Nigel's musical life; one of the most traumatic times was when he changed his mouthpiece at the age of twenty-three. This resulted in him completely wrecking his embouchure and has now spent almost a lifetime searching for a satisfactory replacement, a point he shares with all other brass players to be mindful of.

Achievements have been many, particularly in the recording area of his career with the BBC Radio Orchestra. Nigel, being a modest man, will let his daughter have the say on the question of achievements. For her, the most outstanding musical moment in her father's musical career is playing the theme from Dmitri Tiomkin's 1960 film *The Alamo*. She first heard him play it over twenty years ago and to this day it still sends shivers down her spine.

From his childhood days of brass banding Nigel has fond memories of Christmas carolling round the streets of North Derbyshire. That was back in the 1940s when local people all came out on to the frosty streets to listen. As a youngster playing in the band almost sixty years ago it was a particularly memorable because it was the only time the band had a financial share out from part of the collection money.

Today Nigel is still as busy as ever, working with the BBC Big Band and with the trumpet section. He can be heard on Radio 2 on Monday evenings. For those readers in the Bedfordshire area he leads his own Big Band and can be heard performing at the annual Christmas concert. Nigel says, 'It takes about twelve months' rehearsal to make it sound good!'

He is still grateful for his brass band days: 'It was those early days that gave me my musical start on the road to becoming a professional musician. Those music teachers who I used to pay pennies to have weekly cornet lessons with them, and for sharing their musical knowledge with me, I will always remember and be forever grateful.'

ROWLAND JONES

'At Queensbury he was known as the singing gasman'

Enoch Rowland Jones was born in 1912 and lived in the village of Gwaun-Cae-Gurwen, a small community on the outskirts of Ammanford and a bus ride from Swansea. He was born into a musical family and was the only son of Timothy and Anne Jones, who also had two daughters: Peggy, who was seven years younger than Rowland and died several years ago, and elder sister Nellie Bronwyn.

In 1924 he was introduced and encouraged to play a brass instrument by joining the Gwaun-Cae-Gurwen Silver Band by his uncle, Dan Lloyd, who was the conductor. Like all his contemporaries he too went on to work at Steer Pit, the local mine, but his father felt that Rowland had a gift for music, and found him alternative employment as an engine driver on the surface rather than going under ground.

The Gwaun-Cae-Gurwen Silver Band had a strong history because they had taken part in the National Brass Band Festival contest at the Crystal Palace the year before he was born in 1911. Although the band played off No. 3 under the baton of T.J. Rees they were not amongst the prizes that day. The band followed that visit with another crack at the Nationals the following year, but even though playing off what might have been described as a better draw, No. 10, it was still not amongst the prizes.

Bickershaw Colliery Band in 1946. From left to right, back row: Clifton Jones; William (Bill) Clegg, A. Coultas, Joseph (Joe) Nightingale, Jack Mawdesley, Robert (Bob) Clarke, Edward (Ted) Farrington, Harry Gray, W. Horrabin, Ted Gray (Snr). Middle row: Herbert (Bert) Healy, Peter Gill, Harry Pollard, H. Pownall, J. Gregory, Vince Preston, William (Bill) Gill, Charlie Hulse, J. Mather, E. Nesbitt. Front row: A. Hicks, Jack Wilson, Walter Wilding, Fred Fogarty, William Haydock, Lt-Col Ernest Hart MC, H. Jackson, E. Rowland Jones, William (Bill) Gregory and W. Dawber.

The next time the band appeared at the Crystal Palace was in 1925. Rowland, as one of their youngest members, would never have dreamt that he would one day be a leading instrumentalist at the Crystal Palace, and would rub shoulders with some of the leading names in the brass band world. The band took part again in 1927 but on that visit the band played under the baton of Tal Morris. I believe the last time Rowland played in the championships with his village band was in 1931.

It was not long after that the 'talent scouts' from Yorkshire heard about this rising star euphonium player from the valleys. It was Arthur O. Pearce, the legendary conductor from the Black Dyke Mills Band himself, who took the day-long train journey from his native Queensbury to listen to Rowland in his own backyard at the Gwaun-Cae-Gurwen bandroom. Arthur was sufficiently impressed with what he heard to invite Rowland to travel back up to Yorkshire to audition for the vacant principal euphonium position following the departure of Percy Shaw.

On the 12 March 1934, after a successful audition, he was invited to join the band, which was in good time to appear at the Crystal Palace with his new band under the baton of William Halliwell, performing John Ireland's test piece *Comedy*. That first outing with the band saw it awarded fourth prize, behind the mighty Foden's Motor Works and Fred Mortimer who took the coveted first place. This win completed Foden's 1930s Crystal Palace treble. It was whilst he was with Black Dyke that in addition to playing solo performances on the euphonium Rowland was also invited to sing solos with the band.

During his tenure with Black Dyke it was rarely out of the prizes at the Nationals, although the band never actually took first place during the five years he was with them. Rowland made his last appearance for Black Dyke at the National Finals in 1938. He resigned from the band on 24 March 1939, having been persuaded to join Bickershaw Colliery Band under the baton of William Haydock.

Later in the same year he and two friends visited the Greyhound Inn on the East Lancs' Road to order lunch for Christmas Day. The war had started, and they could not get home for Christmas. Rose Ann was the receptionist who took their lunch order; it was this meeting which was the start of their great and long life together. They were married in Leigh, Lancashire, in September 1941 and made their home at 11 Byron Grove in Leigh at a time when Rowland was working in the pay office at Bickershaw Colliery. This was a busy time for him, working during the day, then on night-watch for the Home Guard and then entertaining the troops with the band during the evening. On top of all that he was taking singing lessons with local singing celebrity Tom Burke. Rowland's ambition at that time was to be an opera singer, something that had been encouraged by Arthur O. Pearce at Black Dyke.

On the contest arena during Rowland's eight year tenure with Bickershaw the band faired well. In 1946 Eric Ball composed his first piece for the Belle Vue September Contest (British Open Championships), *Salute for Freedom*, a piece which could have been written for Bickershaw. The opening called for a lyrical euphonium performance. Rowland Jones led the band to first place before going on to join the Sadler's Wells Opera Company in 1947.

It was whilst he was a member of the Bickershaw Colliery Band that he was first introduced to Tom Burke, who had been a noted professional pre-war tenor singer and someone who was well known at Covent Garden. He had initially heard Rowland sing at one of the Bickershaw band concerts whilst as a member of the audience. It was he who suggested that Rowland should take up singing seriously. Having discovered him it was then Tom who went on to give this amateur tenor the professional tuition that was to give him a new career away from the world of brass bands.

His successful audition for a place at the Sadler's Wells Opera Company was held in July 1946 in Manchester. Having been accepted, he was given his first professional singing role in the following September, making his debut as Turrido in Mascagni's *Cavalleria Rusticana*. His debut was a success, and from then on he was given most of the major tenor roles in the repertory. It has been said that he was at his best in Slavonic roles such as Jenik in *The Bartered Bride* and Lensky in *Eugene Onegin*. These successes saw him being cast for the part of 'Boris' in the first British performance of Janacek's *Katya Kabanova* in 1951. This had never been heard in England until this 1951 performance, and was a major event in the history of British opera. For Sadler's Wells he was their 'Alfred' in almost all their performances of *Die Fledermaus*, a role he was performing when they moved to their new home at the Coliseum Theatre in London.

In 1945 his first daughter Sybil Roishna was born in Leigh, and shortly after moving to Middlesex their second, Sally Reburn, was born in 1952 in Ealing. It was during their time in Middlesex that Roseann bought a sweet shop in Southall to supplement the family income after the war years. From this home they moved to Ruislip (where Rowland was working as a freelance singer with the Welsh National Opera Company, English National Opera Company, Covent Garden Opera Company and at such prestigious venues as the Dublin Grand).

In September 1947 he fulfilled a promise he made to Major Hart at Bickershaw, that he would compete with the band at Belle Vue at the British Open for the last time. He is likely to have been one of the few (if not the only) brass band soloist to both stand up and play an instrumental solo and then perform a vocal solo on the same programme.

He was also a prolific broadcaster for both the BBC and BBC Wales. It was also during this time that he was a singing tutor at the Guildhall School of Music, where he taught many people who themselves were to become well-known professional singers. His successful musical career also included singing at the Proms in London.

On 1 July 1969, along with fifteen other famous Welsh singers, Rowland was invited to perform at the investiture of the Prince of Wales at Caernarfon Castle. This was in front of 4,000 guests inside the medieval walls, with thousands more watching from the dry moat, and millions more from around the world watching on television.

Rowland and Roseann decided to move back to Wales, and during 1972 and 1973 had a house built in Llanrhaeader in Clwyd. This also gave him the opportunity of accepting a post as peripatetic teacher where he taught at Rhyl, Bangor, Chester and Cardiff Castle. In his home he also had a studio where he had a busy schedule teaching private students.

Throughout his career he travelled extensively and was heard singing regularly in many different countries including Germany, Brussels and Turkey. Every year he would perform at the Battle of Britain commemoration in Jersey as the guest artiste.

One of his last performances in Amman Valley was in the oratorio *Elijah*, performed by the Brynaman Old Age Pensioners in 1976. After a lifetime in music this former miner died on 28 August 1978, aged sixty-six.

It was the people of his adopted home in Llanrhaeader who helped to establish the Rowland Jones Award which is presented annually at the National Eisteddfod, an event where he was in regular demand as a judge for the brass and singing sections.

While at Black Dyke he was given a job at the company, just as every other player was in those days. He was employed as the company gasman. He was the man who visited all the mill houses owned by John Foster's, occupied by many employees of the company, to read their gas meters. Even today he is still remembered in Queensbury: the family of a former tenant of John Foster's recalled when he used to call at his grandmother's home, an elderly lady who was blind. Rowland would make his regular call to read the meter and then their grandmother would always make him a cup of tea. He would always reciprocate the kind gesture by singing one of her favourite songs before he left. This saw him become known as 'the singing gasman' throughout the works and village.

As a youngster Geoff Whitham was introduced to Rowland by Arthur O. Pearce's son Harold as a fellow euphonium player. Back in those days young Geoff was a singer in the village church and Rowland would come along to help out by singing the tenor parts.

One of Geoff's most lasting memories of Rowland was back in the days when he was the musical director at Hammonds Sauce Works Band. At one particular concert he contacted and persuaded Rowland to come along and be the guest soloist – being the gentleman, he readily agreed for his old friend, but only on one condition: he would play as long as Geoff played as well. What a night that must have been, when two of the finest euphonium players of their respective generations stood together on the same stage and played Drigo's *Serenade*.

Geoffrey Whitham, former solo euphonium and conductor at Black Dyke Mills Band conductor at Hammond Sauce Works Band

After almost twenty years of not playing a euphonium Rowland had the opportunity whilst visiting the band of picking one up. When asked if he had played recently he informed the gathered audience of old friends, 'No, not for many years.' He was then invited to try out a euphonium from the bandroom upstairs – on his own and in the privacy of the rehearsal room, he did.

Apparently what Rowland did not know at the time was that all his friends could hear every note he played. It is said that even after so long he could play that well-known euphonium solo *Grandfather's Clock* at speed and with clarity.

Memory from the bandroom of the Gwaun-Cae-Gurwen Silver Band

DEREK SOUTHCOTT
'... quick to grasp the nuances of the big band style ...'

I suppose the first time I came across the name of Derek Southcott was on the eve of the British Open Championships at Belle Vue in 1968. The test piece was Gilbert Vinter's *John O'Gaunt*, and Derek was playing second trombone with the Black Dyke Mills Band. Although there was only a handful of us at the traditional pre-contest public rehearsal Black Dyke held in the village, those of us who were there knew this test piece was different. Derek recalls that whenever it was music by Gilbert Vinter they knew to expect something both challenging and different.

The trombone section in those days was Frank Berry, Derek and Ian Copland on bass. For those readers not familiar with the piece, at one point it calls for 'Bell-up' on all three trombone parts. Geoffrey Brand, who was the band's professional conductor and someone who conducted them to many successes, wanted the trombone section to actually stand up at the contest and face the adjudicator's box when it came to play the 'Bell-up' section. At what was a packed Kings Hall that day, with an atmosphere that can only be described as sheer electric, Black Dyke took to the stage with Geoffrey at the helm in what was his first contest outing with the band, everyone anticipated a memorable performance. The rest, as they say, is history: the

Black Dyke Mills Band, early summer 1962. From left to right, back row: Jeffrey Bairstow, Jack Brooke, Leonard Haley, Tommy Waterman, Eric Bland, John Clay, Les Hanman. Middle row: David Summersgill, Grenville Richmond, Derek Southcott, William Gibson, Maurice Murphy, David Pratt, Peter Hey, Sam Smith, Malcolm Blowers, Gordon Sutcliffe, Wally Shaw. Front row: Peter McNab, Charles Emmott, Geoffrey Witham, John Slinger, Jack Emmott, (conductor), Leighton Lucas (professional conductor), John Clough, Brian Broadbent (euphonium), Ernest Keeton, Harry Pickering.

band had the only trombone section to stand up that day, and the band took the coveted first prize with 194 points. Geoffrey Brand has fond memories of that day:

> During the preparation of John O'Gaunt I became increasingly aware that the bold statement of the John O'Gaunt motif at bar 306 – scored for trombones only and marked 'Bell-up' – really had to be commanding and dramatic ... I felt that even Black Dyke's marvellously forthright trombones were not able to produce sufficient volume to really command the scene as the composer had intended.
>
> At the Thursday evening rehearsal, in the Victoria Hall, I decided that to stand up was needed – and having tried it and heard it I knew it worked, so stand up they did. The important point is that the gesture was entirely musically based. Was it a secret? No, not really, since the audience at Victoria Hall saw and heard it all; but I thought it unnecessary to announce it to the world before the actual performance. On the platform at Belle Vue it worked splendidly – and since Black Dyke Mills Band were winners on the day, the means justified the end ...

Derek Southcott was born in 1946 in Hitchin, Hertfordshire. His dad, Ted, was a cockney and his mother, Jessie, was born in Halifax. In the early post-war years ex-servicemen had to look for work. Shortly after Derek's third birthday the family moved north and his mother worked for Crossley's Carpet Mill at Dean Clough in Halifax, while his dad was employed as an auto-electrician at Hoffman's, a well respect garage which was also in Halifax.

When Derek was ten years old and on a family outing he heard Eddie Calvert playing his golden trumpet. Well, Derek made his mind up there and then: 'that's what I want to do.'

Derek was introduced to the world of brass bands through Louis Swingler (the former 1930s Black Dyke horn player), who worked at Dean Clough carpet mill, and who was actively involved with the Crossley Carpets' junior band. Although the golden trumpet never materialised, his first instrument was the baritone; the nearest he came to playing the trumpet was when he moved onto the cornet.

George Ferneyhough, the second trombone player and for a while the Eb bass player for the Crossley's senior band, began teaching him, and it was during those early lessons that George suggested that he should move on to the trombone. Well, to say Derek was made up was an understatement: he was soon telling everyone, even the vicar at his local church, that he was now going to be in church pantomimes and concerts. Such confidence for a twelve year old ...

However, it wasn't long until the initial interest began to fade after he realised that it wasn't going to be as easy as he first thought. However, through dogged perseverance he did stick with it and started to improve. He moved from the Crossley Carpets' junior band to play with the Friendly Band, which was and still is based on the outskirts of Halifax. His next teacher was John Harrison, musical director of the Crossley Carpets' senior band, and a highly respected name in the brass band world.

At the age of fourteen Derek was a regular winner on the slow melody circuits, and was beginning to be known in all the right places. It wasn't long before he was appointed the second trombone position at Crossley Carpets' senior band.

Derek was now receiving tuition at the home of Ronnie Fawthrop, the ex-second trombone player at Black Dyke. It was here that he met Grenville Richmond, the solo trombone player with Black Dyke. In 1961, aged sixteen, he successfully auditioned for the vacant second trombone position at Black Dyke. Grenville decided to leave Black Dyke in 1964 and felt that Derek was good enough to audition for the vacant principal trombone position, but sadly that was not to be.

In Christmas 1969 an unfortunate accident changed his life and future musical direction. Whilst leaving home he slipped on a patch of ice, which necessitated a full-length plaster cast for several weeks. He was unable to sit on the band coach and travel to engagements.

In 1964, he was the 'Champion Trombone of Great Britain', and was also a member of the Champion Quartet. From left to right: Ian Copland, Colin Hardy (who was also the band's second baritone player as well), Peter McNab (conductor), Derek Southcott and Frank Berry.

It was whilst on this enforced break from Black Dyke that he was approached and offered the opportunity of playing in a pit orchestra for an amateur show in Huddersfield. This was where he met the trumpet player Brian Tann, a player who had been around the show scene for a number of years. Brian introduced Derek to the Batley Variety Club 'Blow Band' which was the 'Stuart Atkins' Orchestra', the club's regular orchestra, where he was asked to join on trombone. Little did he know he was now on the fringe of a new musical career, taking the first steps along a road to becoming a professional musician.

It was now 1972, and Derek's work commitments were growing. He was still a member of Black Dyke, playing with local pit orchestras, playing at Batley Variety Club and still holding down his daytime job as an engineering draughtsman. A busy young man to say the least, and something had to give. He had now made his mind up to become a professional musician, a decision that prompted him to resign from Black Dyke after nine years, an experience and time which he still appreciates were musically very profitable.

At Batley Variety Club he came into contact with many professional musicians, one of those was Stuart Atkins, trombone player in the club's small band, and someone who Derek was to ultimately 'dep' for on a number of occasions. It was also through his contact and help from Stuart that he became a member of the club's 'amalgamated band'. This band was formed on the occasions when the big stars of the day were performing at the club, such as Johnny Mathis, Shirley Bassey, Jack Jones, the Three Degrees and Cliff Richard but to name a few.

Stuart quickly realised that Derek was a good player, and he recalls that in those early days Derek had to be encouraged. However, when the orchestra's lead trombone player left, Stuart took him aside and taught him all he knew about leading a section and phrasing. Derek was quick to grasp the nuances of the big band style of phrasing. Before long, Derek was invited to join the Wakefield Theatre Club by Willey Hurst, the band leader. He took some sound advice from Stuart, who said, 'If you are going to turn pro, this is as good an offer as you could get,' because you would be playing second trombone alongside Eddie Hargreaves (a top trombone

Christopher Houlding (standing to the right of Derek Southcott in the centre) was the musical director of Stocksbridge Band, who accompanied Derek for his 1993 CD recording, 'The Many Sounds of Derek Southcott: Facets'. Also featured on this recording was the Derek Southcott sextet.

player in those days), the lead trombone player at the theatre club orchestra. Stuart is very proud of Derek because he went on to be a member of the BBC's Northern Dance Orchestra which led to him being invited to join the Syd Lawrence Orchestra and being a member for twenty-two years. (In 2007, Stuart launched his debut book, *Swinging with the Stars*.)

Derek was now embarking on the road of the professional musician and was actively looking to build up the amount of freelance work he was beginning to be offered. In 1972 he and James Shepherd had been discussing the possibility of forming a small group similar to that of the Black Dyke Octet. The group would not simply play brass band music but it would expand its repertoire to cover a wider range of music. Those who made up the original James Shepherd Versatile Brass included: Jim Shepherd (cornet and trumpet), David Horsfield (flugel horn, cornet and trumpet), Peter Ferris (trumpet), Brian Wood (horn), David Moore (euphonium), Derek Southcott (trombone), Donald Bowes (bass trombone), Colin Aspinall (tuba), Harvey Whiteley (percussion). Shortly after the group's first successful concert (held at the Uppermill Civic Hall), Derek was then offered a full-time position at the Wakefield Theatre Club, so after being with the JSVB from its inception he now had to leave.

Whilst playing at the Wakefield Theatre Club he met Ernie Watson, who was the lead trumpet at the BBC Northern Dance Orchestra. Derek is certain that meeting Ernie changed his musical direction and put him on a path that today. It was Ernie who gave Derek a gentle nudge and said, 'go for it ...' One of fifty-three applicants for the job, his audition proved successful, and following this appointment he left his job and became a full-time musician. It was whilst playing with the BBC Northern Radio Orchestra that he was asked to 'dep' with the famous Syd Lawrence Orchestra on lead trombone. This situation worked out well for Derek because Lawrence believed that the paying public only wanted to socialise on Friday, Saturday and Sunday nights, and on that basis he rarely if ever took any engagements during the week – thus enabling Derek to maintain his BBC commitments and his new work with Syd Lawrence. After twenty-two years of playing in the Syd Lawrence Orchestra Derek decided it was time to retire.

6

THE COMPOSERS

*Frank Wright MBE, champion cornet player, conductor,
composer, arranger and adjudicator.*

FRANK WRIGHT
'Australian Cornet Champion'

Frank Wright (front left) and Percy Code (front right), two of Australia's finest cornet players, are shown with C. Sheehan (euphonium) and E. Jones (horn) in this City of Ballarat Band quartet. (Courtesy of Gavin Holman at www.ibew.co.uk)

Frank Wright was born in the old gold mining town of Smeaton, near Ballarat, Australia on 2 August 1901, and throughout his life he embraced everything the brass band world had to offer both in Australia and Britain (where he lived from 1933 until his death on 16 November 1970).

From an early age his parents, William and Sarah, encouraged music interests, This meant that Frank was given piano lessons, taught composition and orchestration. He was then taught to play the cornet by Percy Code, the famous cornet player and conductor of the City of Ballarat Municipal Band. At the age of nineteen Frank Wright matched Percy's achievement by becoming the Australian Cornet Champion, and the following year took over from him as conductor of the band.

Frank left Australia in 1933 and the following year had been appointed the conductor of St Hilda's Professional Band for its 1934 concert season. In 1935 he was appointed music director (parks department) at the London County Council. This was the start of his total involvement in the UK music scene. From 1934 to 1969 he was seen regularly as an adjudicator at the National Finals. He was often asked to adjudicate at many other contests throughout the country. He transcribed some of the best known test pieces from the mid-1950s to his final transcription, *Benvenuto Cellini*, just before his death in 1970.

He was awarded the MBE and was a member of the Worshipful Company of Musicians from the late 1950s. Just before his death the company made him a Master.

When I moved to Watford ... I was appointed treasurer of the London and Southern Counties Area Committee and also a member of the National Contesting Council. It was during this time that I regularly came in contact with Frank Wright, who had been adjudicating at the London Finals since 1945. I got to know him well and considered him to be a friend. I visited him quite often at his office which overlooked Trafalgar Square. We often talked about his admiration for Dame Nellie Melba, and his rare collection of cylinder recordings, a collection that was eventually to be sold off at Christies, the London auction house.
Bram Thompson, solo horn Scottish CWS Band 1949-1963

RAY STEADMAN-ALLEN

'As a child I had no musical ambitions'

The first time I became aware of Lt-Col Ray Steadman-Allen was back in 1983 when his composition *Stantonbury Festival* was the third section Yorkshire area test piece. This was a good year for us at my old band, Clifton and Lightcliffe, and for conductor John Edward. The band was awarded second place and qualified to play in the Nationals; this also proved lucky for us because all four sections played at the Royal Albert Hall. Since then I have played many more of his compositions for lower section bands and I say with confidence that if his name is at the top of the score then you know it will be a wonderful piece of music to play and will be equally enjoyable for the audience to listen to.

Ray Steadman-Allen was the elder son of Salvation Army officers Frederick and Gladys Allen and was born in September 1922 at the Salvation Army 'Mothers' Hospital' in Clapton, East London. Twins David (now deceased) and his sister Vida were born nine years later.

Children of Salvation Army officers inevitably move house on many occasions during their parents' years of service, and the Allens were no exception. When he was a child living in Barnsley his mother was taking piano lessons and thought it a good idea that young Ray should go along too. His dad had played the trombone whilst as a member of the Chatteris SA Band in 1910. So it was inevitable that Ray would be asked which instrument he was going to play.

His earliest memory of a brass band was in 1928 when the family lived in Malvern, which had a good SA Band in those days, but with the joining age being seven Ray could only sit on the sidelines watching the band perform. However, he does recall being allowed to 'march' behind the band pretending to play a cornet, holding on to an old 'parp-parp' air motor horn. He didn't have proper cornet tuition for another four years. The first band piece he can consciously remember was in the Harry Kirk's composition *Steadily Forward March*, a fine old road march, played by the west London Norland Castle Band in 1929, in Birmingham. It was whilst living in Barnsley that he had his first lesson on a cornet, but like so many other youngsters he had problems playing notes in the upper register. However, the following year, when the family had moved to West Hartlepool, he was given the opportunity of following in his father's footsteps by playing the trombone.

His very early musical education was largely through an excellent music master (organist) at school. Aside from his musical composition he has always enjoyed reading, military history, writing, gardening and has even dabbled a bit with painting and playing the viola. As a member of the youth band in West Hartlepool he played the piano accompaniments for the soloists on the programmes. As a change from the classical pieces of music he tried his hand at transcribing some band pieces, and this helped him with the instrumentation and was the beginning of a life in brass band composition. In 1937 he started working at the Salvation Army International Headquarters as an office boy to General Evangeline Booth, daughter of the Salvation Army's founder. He joined the band and choir at Harlesden, and began writing for a small instrumental group made up of the band's teenagers.

The first piece he submitted to a music publisher was a selection which he called *Glory, Laud and Honour*. It was rejected. However, by the time he was nineteen he had already written his second piece, *Bethlehem Suite*, which he had written whilst wartime fire-watching in Rugby. In 1945 he had the satisfaction of hearing this piece performed by the International Staff Band in Glasgow. This composition was finally published after the war but was not his first commercially published piece: that distinction went to a march which he titled *Gladsome Morn*. During his navy service (1942-1945) in the Persian Gulf he even found time to write some piano pieces and it was there where he began experimenting with orchestral compositions. In his early years he had a number of musical heroes. These included Arthur Sullivan, Vaughan Williams, Debussy and the child prodigy Constant Lambert.

After a bandmaster's correspondence course, he went on to pass the brass band conducting LTCL (Licentiate of Trinity College, London) diploma in Glasgow with the Scottish CWS Band; the distinguished composer Sir Granville Bantock was the examiner. During their meeting he told Ray of his connections with Paxton's music publishers and discussed with him, for quite a long time, his hopes and aspirations for the future. As they went their separate ways Sir Granville handed Ray one of his cards and said, 'Come and see me after the war.' Sadly that meeting never took place – Sir Granville died in October 1946 – but Ray still has the card he gave him.

Having been encouraged by Sir Granville Bantock, he began to think more positively about the world of music. Towards the end of the war he even explored the possibilities of writing film music but without any experience and with so many professionals returning from their own war service and looking for jobs in 'Civvy Street', prospects in that field looked bleak.

In 1946 he was invited to join the staff of the Salvationist Publishing and Supplies International Music Editorial Department, and in 1949 was appointed an officer at the Harrow Corps. In 1960 the newly acquired publisher Wright & Round appointed him the new managing editor, a position he held for about a year, and it was during his time at Wright & Round's that he produced his *120 Hymn Tunes for Brass Band* books; these of course are known throughout the brass band world as 'the Red Hymn Books'. After spending a year at Wright & Round's he went back to the Supplies International Music Editorial Department in London and then in 1967 he was appointed as the new head of the department, a position he held for twenty-three years.

It has been written that his creative genius was ahead of its time and was instrumental in guiding the Salvation Army's music into previously uncharted areas during his tenure at the International Music Department. Before his retirement in 1987, he worked in Australia (from 1980 to 1983), and on his return he was appointed the editor of the Salvation Army's musical weekly *The Musician*, a position he held until he retired. Whilst he was no stranger to tight deadlines, the constant demands of producing a weekly were a struggle.

With age comes maturity and Ray's musical tastes began to change. Rather than musical heroes, he now has an appreciation and an affectionate respect for friends such as Wilfred Heaton, an appreciation of Professor Philip Wilby and Professor Edward Gregson and for Dr Kenneth Downie. He had the privilege of both encouraging and publishing their first works. There are four American composers he also had similar connections with, and are all now eminent professional composers: James Curnow, Bruce Broughton, William Himes and Stephen

Taken at Harlesden, c. 1939. From left to right: Russell Sinhock, Ken White, Norman Johnson, Stan Burnham (killed in the RAF during the Second World War), Norman Mead and Ray Steadman-Allen (who enjoyed a short period in the ISB after the war).

Bulla. He has gained a great deal over the years from many diverse composers and musicians, including Brahms, Sibelius and, from the modern era, E.J. Moeran, the English composer and Arvo Pärt, Estonia's most renowned composer. In the band world the compositions of Eric Ball also played an important role in the development of his own compositions.

Inevitably, as with all musicians, there have been those lighter moments and Ray has both seen and experienced many. Probably the earliest was as a youngster in the days when the family home was used as a storage facility for all kinds of brass instruments. He recalls trying to blow a baritone, with disastrous results. His father said, 'Put the temptation out of the way.' This one sentence convinced him for quite sometime afterwards that a baritone was in fact called a 'temptation'. One rather more 'toe-curling' incident came when he was preparing his 800+ tune book. By 1983 Ray was busy co-ordinating and proofing the final stages, to meet the engravers' deadlines, when he discovered that *Westminster Abbey* by Purcell, one of his all time favourite hymns, had been left out. Luckily, however, the engravers discovered there was a space at the end of the book indicating something was missing, so *Westminster Abbey* was unofficially added.

Ray can look back over a lifetime of creating wonderful music that will stand the test of time. Throughout his fifty-seven years of married life he has had the love and tireless support of his wife Joy and then that of his two daughters (Revd) Barbara and (Recruiting Sergeant) Rosemary (Chatham SA and member of the International Staff Songsters). One event involving Joy that Ray particularly recalls was when he was scheduled to conduct a massed chorus at the Royal Albert Hall, which coincided with their wedding anniversary. On arriving at the pre-concert rehearsal he suddenly realised he had forgotten the score. Without hesitation Joy went back home to pick it up and was back at the rehearsal in good time. Ray was standing at the podium, with the massed chorus before him, when he opened the score, baton ready in hand. In large block capitals he saw the words 'JOY LOVES RAY. HAPPY ANNIVERSARY'.

Looking back over his life, I asked Ray if he had achieved all his ambitions. 'As a child I had no musical ambitions; in my early teens my interests lay more in chemistry and the sciences.

This included performing very simple experiments at home.' Are there any lost ambitions in his adult life? 'Conducting is something I would loved to have done more of – the opportunity of interpreting the work of others would have been wonderful – but being offered on rare occasions the opportunity of being a guest conductor has made up for those missed opportunities.'

His music catalogue totals over 200 compositions principally for brass bands and Salvation Army Bands, which includes a number of contest test pieces such as; *Seascapes* for the 1988 National Finals, *Victorian Snapshots*, *On Ratcliff Highway* the 2007 first section, *Chorale* for the 1991 second section and *Amaranth* for the 1992 third section. Along with numerous choral works and many pieces that remain in manuscript form. These pieces have been generally written for recordings or special concert presentations.

In 2005, 'R.S.A.' as he is known by all his friends was admitted to the Order of the Founder, the highest honour that the Salvation Army can bestow on one of its members. Ray Steadman-Allen, whilst always being characteristically modest about his achievements, has been described on many occasions as the Salvation Army's most creative talent.

I first met Ray when he was an editor in the Salvation Army's music editorial department. He was very encouraging about my early writing which helped to give me much-needed confidence.

The main influence on me was his music. All through my childhood I heard it: *The Veterans*, *The Eternal Quest*, *Go Down Moses*, and many marches, including *Exultation*. The biggest impact came with *The Holy War*. It came out in 1965, when I was a student at the Royal College in Manchester. It definitely put down a marker for a new generation of composers. Many other landmark works followed, including *Logos 1*, *On Ratcliffe Highway*, and *The Lord is King!*

Apart from these larger works, I am constantly amazed and grateful for the example Ray provides of how to produce music for everyday use, which always shows character, invention and personality.

Dr Kenneth Downie, who has been writing music of quality for over forty years

---

My first recollection of the music, as a young teenage boy, was *The Holy War*. I heard it at Star Lake Musicamp. This music made a huge impact and I asked my father – a member of the New York Staff Band at the time – if he could find me a copy of the score. Soon after, he came home from THQ [Territorial Headquarters] with a copy. I took it to the piano and tried to rediscover the beautiful sounds, and by so doing I had my first experience close up with this wonderful masterpiece. To this day, it never grows old for me.

My first connection with the man was shortly after the 'discovery' mentioned above. I decided to write to the composer. In those days there was no internet, no email, and it was more of a wild idea to contact a composer than it would be now. To my amazement, Captain Ray Steadman-Allen wrote back a kind note of encouragement to this young unknown lad dabbling with one of his many compositions at the piano. Some years later we finally met when he was a guest at Star Lake and the friendship and mentorship grew from that time.

Lastly, I should say that it's impossible to know how deep RSA's impact on shaping my life's path may be. It certainly ignited a spark of curiosity about the idea of sounds jumping off a score page. And the encouragement at a tender age can not be overlooked. Through the years I've never been far from an RSA score, having played so many of the classics in bands throughout my SA associations. All have been worth the closer look. I sincerely thank him for his friendship and influence across the decades.

Stephen Bulla, chief arranger to the President's Own US Marine Band and White House Orchestra

J.A. GREENWOOD
'Even the diehards were beginning to fear him'

Look through almost any band's music library and you will find literally stacks of music that is not played anymore and in many cases is unlikely to be ever played again. This includes music from both composers whose music was very popular for a short time and the household-name composers whose music was once played at almost every own choice contest, and was a 'cert' on every band's concert programme for years, before it too became unfashionable.

Some of the pieces I played almost fifty years ago in our third (but more often fourth) section band included the Eduardo Brepsant march *Belphegor*, the old overture *Caliph of Baghdad*, Albert Ketelbey's *In a Persian Market* – and what about the *Community Land* selections and music from the shows of the 1940s and '50s? Then there are the solos that are not played either; when was the last time you heard William Rimmer's cornet solo *Click Clack Polka*, or the John Hartmann's euphonium solo *Weidekhr*? Times have certainly moved on: 'play to the audience,' as our old bandmaster used to say. When, for example, was the last time your band played a piece of music written by one of the most prolific of brass band composers and arrangers, J.A. Greenwood?

I am sure that the ones most readers, particularly trombone players, will know are his trombone solos *The Acrobat*, which he composed in 1935 and which was followed in 1936 with *The Jester*, both pieces becoming firm favourites for player and audience alike. Both of these solos were introduced to a wider audience in March 1939 when they were recorded by Jack Pinches and Black Dyke Mills Band on the HMV record label.

John (or Jonny, as he was known to his closest friends) Ambrose Greenwood was born in 1876 in Winsford, Cheshire, the son of Thomas, a carpenter, and Marie, a professional actress. There appears to be few records of his early years in the world of brass bands, but what there is reveals that he was initially taught to play the cornet by his father. By the time

August 1935 at St Catherine's Church, Tranmere. John Ambrose Greenwood and his wife Fanny (née Bourne) on the extreme right-hand side pose with (from left to right): Mr and Mrs Solomon Butler, -?-, Edith Butler (groom's mother), Norman Butler (groom), Viola (bride) and Dorothy (bride's sister).

he was eighteen years old he was playing solo cornet for the Gossages Soap Works Band, Widnes. This band first appeared at the National Finals at the Crystal Palace in 1906 and was one of eight bands that William Rimmer conducted at that year's contest. Although Gossages were not placed he still conducted the first four placed bands. After some success Gossages' time had come and gone, and by the First World War it was another band that had faded into the mists of time. John Greenwood's first band as a trainer was Crosby St Luke's, which brought him to the attention of other bands.

In 1899 John Greenwood was playing second cornet at the New Brighton Orchestra. Looking through the *Liverpool Echo* report of a concert that was held at New Brighton Tower in May of that year, his fellow musicians included J.G. Dobbing on first cornet and H. Bantock who was playing first violin. Sunderland-born J.G. Dobbing is a name that may be familiar to the followers of the Cory Band: he conducted the band at their first September Contest (what we know today as the British Open Brass Band Championship) in 1922. Violinist Herman Bantock was the brother of (Sir) Granville Bantock, who brought a number of pieces to the brass band repertoire.

John Greenwood went on to play with a number of the top bands at the turn of the century as a solo cornetist after the New Brighton Tower went bankrupt in 1900. He was also advised to turn professional, going on to play solo cornet at Pemberton Old, Crooke and Wingates Bands, under John Gladney, Alexander Own and William Rimmer. In 1906 his name appeared for the first time at the September Contest at Belle Vue when he conducted Palmer's Prize Band, a band that was associated with the Palmer's Shipbuilding & Iron Co. (Hebburn & Jarrow on Tyne). Although they were not placed, the following year he conducted them at the National Brass Band Championships at the Crystal Palace.

By 1910 he was conducting Hebden Bridge Band at both the September Contest and at the Crystal Palace. Another band he conducted at Crystal Palace that day was an unsuccessful St Hilda's Colliery Band. In 1911 he was conducting the Horwich RMI Band, but it was 1912 when, as one of the leading professional conductors, he accepted a position at Black Dyke Mills Band, a position he held until 1921.

These were golden years for John Greenwood – and he was not only engaged to conduct the top-flight bands either. In 1910, whilst conducting three of the championship section bands (Hebden Bridge, King Cross and St Hilda's), he also conducted three sections below at the Percy Main (NER) Band. In 1934 at the Crystal Palace National Championships whilst conducting the Manchester-based Baxendale's Band (and then Creswell Colliery Band) in the Grand Shield Contest, he also conducted Crookhall Colliery Welfare Band in the section below and then, one more section below that, he conducted Manchester CWS Tobacco Band and the Newcastle Corporation Tramways Band. Back in those days, he would have been one of the railway company's best customers, dashing backwards and forward to the many rehearsals he would have attended.

During the Second World War Baxendale's was bombed, which saw not only the loss of the company but the band's instruments, music and all their equipment. There was some talk of restarting the band, but it never happened. Some of the former players from Baxendale's Band later joined a new revitalised CWS (Manchester) Band.

Whilst conducting the leading bands, he was considered to be a very hard task master. In 1925 he was engaged to conduct the Marsden Colliery Band at the Crystal Palace Contest. The test piece for that year was Dennis Wright's *Joan of Arc* and things were not going well at all. The pits were on strike so the band rehearsed morning, noon and night. As the frustration set in he was losing patience with the band to such an extent even the die-hards were beginning to feel his wrath and began to fear him.

After the Second World War he devoted most of his time to composition, arranging and adjudicating at contests. His two most famous solos were *The Acrobat* and *The Jester*. Grenville Richmond, the former solo trombone player at Black Dyke Mills Band, remembers playing *The Acrobat* many times. 'This solo usually followed a ballad – something that was completely

Professional conductor John A. Greenwood at a rehearsal with Baxendale's Works Band, c. 1936. This band had a degree of national success in the 1930s and attracted other notable conductors, including Fred Mortimer and his son Harry. Baxendale's best result was in 1933 at the September Belle Vue Contest, playing Princess Nada.

I remember the day when an elderly white-haired gentleman came to our bandroom. It was J.A.Greenwood, who had been asked to conduct the band in the late 1940s – I have vivid memories of the day Mr Greenwood was at the rehearsal. I recall in particular when he asked the back row cornets to play their parts (Eric Ball's test piece *Divertimento*) – after a few moments of listening to their efforts, and after some careful thought, he looked at me on the second cornet chair, then aged eleven, and said 'Is that cornet insured, lad?' Not knowing what to say, I just sat open mouthed, staring at him. Mr Greenwood then said 'If it is insured, lad, chuck it under a bus and get yourself a new one.'
Derek Mitchell, former player and conductor of the City of Chester Band

James Scott, who was a fine cornet player (and retired from playing far too soon, in 1960), can recall one occasion in 1947 after he had left Grimethorpe and before he joined Munn and Felton's Band. (For a short while, which included the 1947 Belle Vue September contest, he was also principal cornet at Ransome and Marles Band.)

David Aspinall, the conductor, knew John Greenwood and asked him to come and run the band through that year's test piece, Dr Richard Maldwyn Price's *Henry V*. The band members had been warned that Mr Greenwood could be a martinet and to take note that if he began to jingle his Albert watch chain between his fingers to beware, because someone was about to cop it. He was very methodical and paid meticulous attention to detail.
James Scott, retired cornet player, conductor and adjudicator

different. This was the kind of solo where you could have some fun with the audience ...'
On one occasion Grenville was playing the solo at a senior citizens gathering in Bradford as
a member of the Black Dyke Mills Octet. One lady on the front row was so taken with his
performance that halfway through she began to laugh. In fact, she laughed so hard that her
false teeth shot out of her mouth, and someone had to catch them before they landed on the
stage. With the exception of cornet player Jack Brook and Grenville, the remaining six members
of the octet couldn't play for laughing.

Another former trombone star, John Maines, also has a happy memory of playing *The
Acrobat*, back in 1962 when he was a member of the Wigan Boys' Club Band. He had played
the solo on a number of occasions and at a concert in Mesnes Park in Wigan he started to
show off a bit. Everything was fine until, during the big downward glissando at the end, the
trombone slide slipped out of his fingers and fell off the end and clattered across the concrete
in front of the bandstand. It was hilarious – that was until bandmaster Mr William Haydock
told John's dad ... To hear *The Acrobat* today always reminds John of his dad's reaction when
told about what had happened, and the back of his dad's hand!

During his life John Greenwood produced over 200 pieces for brass bands from marches to
selections, transcriptions and solos. His last big engagement as an adjudicator was in 1953 as
one of the adjudicators at the National Brass Band Championships at Empress Hall at Earls Court.

After a life in brass bands, at the age of seventy-seven he died, whilst composing a new
overture at his home in Northwood Park, Prenton, Birkenhead. He left four daughters and
three sons. It was recorded in his obituary that 'he was truly a self-taught musician apart from
some lessons in harmony and counterpoint from a teacher outside the brass band movement;
he trod his own path, picking up knowledge where ever he could.' This knowledge he applied
to his own playing and later in his teaching – which led him to become one of the finest brass
band teachers that ever lived, a tip-top adjudicator and a really great composer and arranger
for brass bands. Just remember those words the next time you hear or play *The Acrobat* or *The
Jester*.

The late Bill 'Boy' Blackett, one of the trombone players at Marsden Colliery Band, recalled
in Arthur Taylor's book *Labour and Love* that it was Tommy Frame, the band's solo trombone
player, who always seemed to cop it when professional conductor John A. Greenwood came
to take the rehearsals before a big contest. This was never more so than before the 1925
National Finals in London. With local rivals Harton Colliery and St Hilda's all vying with
each other, local enthusiasm was at fever pitch.

Marsden travelled to London on the early morning train – John Greenwood was already
there because he had been engaged to also conduct Creswell Colliery Band, and he expected
to do well with them, having just taken them to the top spot at Belle Vue. At the pre-contest
rehearsal he was once again very hard on the trombone section, so much so that one player
was crying. After the rehearsal they'd had enough: he was upsetting players so much that the
outcome from a players' meeting decided that he would not be taking them to the contest and
would be replaced by Jack Boddice (and someone else would have to play Jack's euphonium).

The band drew No.4 – following Foden's. Foden's played brilliantly, so much so the applause
went on for almost twenty minutes. At the last moment out strode Johnny Greenwood, and
picked up the baton. Marsden's performance, to use a more modern description, blew every
other band's performance away, even the mighty Foden's. It was Marsden's day, and John
Greenwood's finest hour – and all was forgiven. That 1925 contest had seventeen bands taking
part: three were conducted by John Greenwood and eight were conducted by William Halliwell.

William (Bill) Blackett, Marsden Colliery Band and St Hilda's Professional Band

PHILIP SPARKE

'Someone who can inject fresh vigour into the repertoire'

It is a rare concert these days that does not have at least one piece on the programme that Philip Sparke has composed or arranged: he has been firmly established as one of the most successful composers and arrangers for brass bands over the last thirty years .

He was born in London, and whilst his parents didn't play musical instruments, his father had a fine collection of scratchy old 78s. As a child he was taught to play the recorder and then had violin lessons at school, and he later taught himself to play the trumpet. His earliest recollection of musical composition was after the family had inherited a piano, and he can remember sitting at the keyboard composing a few simple tunes.

He became aware of brass band music quite by chance when he was about twenty and playing in a pit orchestra with a percussionist who played with the Hendon Band, back in the days when it was conducted by Don Morrison. He was taken to the band's rehearsal and liked what he heard, so he wrote a piece of music for them. Not only did they play it, but they liked it as well. He went on to study composition, trumpet and the piano at the Royal College of Music, where he was awarded an ARCM. It was during his days at the college, under the guidance of Professor Philip Canon, that he took a real interest in bands. He joined the college wind orchestra and formed his own brass band from amongst his fellow students.

He first came into wider prominence in 1975 when he entered a competition which was organised by the National Schools Brass Band Association for composers. The competition was judged by a group of well-known composers and was chaired by the British composer Sir Lennox Berkley. Four works were chosen to be performed and judged at the National Festival, at a prestigious venue. The winning composition was *Concert Overture*, written by Philip; the first prize was £500. (His composition had its name changed later to *The Prizewinners*.)

In 1979 he was commissioned by the New Zealand Brass Band Association to write the 1980 National Championships' test piece. The outcome was the wonderful piece *Land of the Long White Cloud*, which was also chosen as the set test piece for the European Championships the same year. Over the next ten years the number of commissioned pieces he was asked to write grew, and his output of fine concert music was receiving equally deserved recognition. By the mid-1980s he had over fifty compositions to his name, which included the 1984 test piece for the Dutch national brass band championships, as well as both Area and National Championship pieces here in the UK. In 1984 he wrote what is arguably his best piece *Year of the Dragon*, and his catalogue of successful contest pieces has increased enormously since then.

During the 1980s he was also the conductor of the Hillingdon Band (now the Denham Hendon Band), and he is now the band president. In 1990 Philip was appointed as the composer-in-residence at what is now the University of Salford). In September 2000 he was awarded the Iles Medal of the Worshipful Company of Musicians for his services to brass bands, something he looks back on as a great honour. Today, he is as busy as ever both at home and abroad, not only as a composer but with guest conducting and adjudicating.

PETER GRAHAM

'A spectacularly imaginative and innovative talent'

Peter Graham has been referred to as the new Eric Ball, a reference he finds very flattering. He certainly lists him as being a writer who, along with Edward Gregson and Ray Steadman-Allen, has had a huge influence in his musical development.

Born in Lanarkshire, Peter came from a musical family and was introduced to both the piano and the world of brass instruments at a very early age through his parents. His father was the bandmaster at the local Salvation Army band in Ayr, on the west coast of Scotland.

With the encouragement of his parents, he went to study music at Edinburgh University, Moray House College, where he graduated in 1980. It was during this period that he became the youngest composer to be commissioned to write the National Brass Band Final's test piece, for the Royal Albert Hall. His composition *Connotations* was a real test for all the bands, a test that saw Black Dyke Mills Band awarded first place, a clear five points ahead of the second-placed band. He has since attained a MMus degree, and a PhD in Composition. Between 1983 and 1986 he lived in New York City, working as a freelance composer and arranger, and was the publications editor with the Salvation Army Music Bureau.

It was also in 1983 that his first big brass band piece, *Dimensions*, was published, and since the success of that piece he has created a special niche for himself in this musical genre. This piece is still played regularly as many lower section bands choose it as an 'own choice' test piece at contests. On his return from New York he soon developed into one of the rising stars of brass band composition. Following the success and acclaim of 'Dimensions', other pieces soon followed, notably *Essence of Time*, *Montage*, *On Alderley Edge*, and *Journey to the Centre of the Earth*, which were all used in National Brass Band Championship Contests, from North America to New Zealand, across Europe and of course here in the UK.

Peter's work did not just include music for brass bands: he has worked regularly as an arranger for television and radio. He has for many years been a leading member of the BBC's *Songs of Praise*, contributing to over forty programmes. He has also written extensively for wind bands including the Tokyo Kosei Wind Orchestra and the Royal Norwegian Navy Band. He was awarded the American Bandmasters Association's prestigious Ostwald Prize for Original Composition for Symphonic Winds in 2002, a great honour, for his composition *Harrison's Dream*. This piece was originally commissioned by the United States Air Force Band, which is based in Washington DC. In 2002, *Harrison's Dream* was used at the National Brass Band Championships at the Royal Albert Hall and was won by the Buy As You View Cory Band. It is still one of the most popular top-section test and own pieces in banding today.

There is rarely a concert performed these days that does not have a Peter Graham composition on the programme. His concert repertoire is very extensive and he is one of those composers who can produce music that both the player and the audience will really enjoy. His music now is truly global, with performances being heard in practically every major country played by some of the best orchestras in the world.

GEOFFREY BRAND

'A life of music'

Geoffrey Brand has lived a life of music: he was born into a Salvation Army family in Gloucester, took his place in the local band and then, at the age of eighteen, won an Open Scholarship to the Royal Academy of Music in London. He went on to play the trumpet with the Royal Philharmonic Orchestra and Covent Garden Orchestra, and in 1955 he joined the BBC as a music producer.

One of his earliest opportunities to conduct a brass band as its professional conductor came in 1962 with the John Dickinson (Aspley) Band (now the Hemel Hempstead Band). In 1967 he became the professional conductor of the famous Black Dyke Mills Band, winning several major contests, including the World Championship in 1970. Today, with son Michael, he runs the very successful music publishing company G & M Brand Publications.

Geoffrey as the new professional conductor at the John Dickinson (Aspley) Band in 1962. Geoffrey is in the front row, fourth from the right.

AFTERWORD

What a fascinating title for a book! My first, and overiding, feeling is one of delight that amongst the list of persons chosen by Chris Helme, whose selection he justifies as 'people who have produced time after time what can only be described as truly magical moments in a performance' some are or were people I have known personally. Thus, through my own connections with the 'world of brass bands' I have been privileged to observe, appreciate and admire their 'specialness'.

I'm delighted also that a chapter about female players is included in this very readable book. Nowadays, not only as brass players, but as composers, arrangers, conductors, organisers, editors, indeed in every possible manner as contributors, ladies play an equal part – and sometimes more than equal!

So where does it all start? The chapter headed 'A Family Affair' touches on the fascinating issues of influences. Even before we enter this world the matter of chance – when, where, and to whom we are born – comes into play. Think for a few moments of your own earliest recollections of the sound of music. Was there singing or were instruments played where you lived; did musical sounds linger in your thoughts and ears after they had ended; when were you first fascinated by the uniqueness of the sounds you heard?

It's that uniqueness of sound which a good brass band can make which has, over the years, lured, enticed and captivated countless thousands to become devotees, enthusiasts, supporters and, essentially, participants in brass band music-making. And, as the author relates, included in those thousands will be those unique few who, through their instruments, will produce sounds which offer a clearer meaning and understanding of a composer's message and concept.

Doubtless, amongst readers of this fascinating book there will be those who through aptitude, application and perseverance *could* – no guarantee is possible – justify consideration for inclusion in a future volume of *What Brass Bands Did For Me*.

Only you, and time, will decide.

Geoffrey Brand, ARAM, LRAM, ARCM

Geoffrey Brand (right) with Dr Roy Newsome (resident conductor, left) and Peter Lambert (managing director of John Foster & Sons, centre) after Black Dyke Mills Band had once again won the National Brass Band Champions of Great Britain, 1967.

MEET THE AUTHOR

For thirty years Chris was a serving police officer, and was awarded the British Empire Medal in 1990 for his service in the community. Over the last twenty-five years, he has written a number of local history books. Whilst some have been commissioned books, a number of others have been self-published.

He has written a weekly nostalgia column in the *Brighouse Echo* weekly newspaper for over twenty-three years, and has produced a sixty-minute nostalgia cassette tape based on a number of the stories from his column. Some of his nostalgic stories have also been published in regional magazines. For over twenty-five years, he taught local history at Adult Community Learning Classes.

Chris joined his first brass band in 1960, and has been both a player and held a number of the administrative roles connected with a brass band. He has been in demand as a speaker for many years, and so in 1997 he published the first edition of his *West Yorkshire Speaker Directory*. The book contained over 150 speakers, presenters, slide-show hosts and a small group of musical entertainers. This directory has now become a bi-annual publication with the current 2009/2010 West, and the additional editions for North and South Yorkshire now also available. (These publications are available through Waterstone's, Amazon and other online book stores.)

He regularly contributed to *Brass Review*, a specialist brass band magazine published by Kirklees Music in Brighouse, and the very successful www.4barsrest.com brass band website. For the last two years, Chris has also written brass band nostalgia stories for the *British Bandsman* magazine. His stories of brass band nostalgia are about some of the personalities and bands from yesteryear, and have proved to be very popular.

For over two years Chris has been the editor of *The Conductor*, the in-house magazine for the National Association of Brass Band Conductors (www.nabbc.org.uk). Chris is also an editor for the *Calderdale Talking Newspaper*, a quarterly magazine tape which is a blend of nostalgia, memories and tales of how life used to be – a mixture well appreciated by all his listeners. He is also the producer and presenter of *Sunday Bandstand*, 2 p.m. to 3 p.m. (UK time) every Sunday on Phoenix FM 96.7 (for listeners beyond Calderdale it is accessible via the internet, www.phoenixfm.co.uk).

Other titles published by The History Press

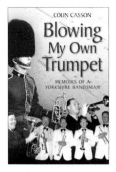

Blowing My Own Trumpet
COLIN CASSON

This charming collection of tales from Haworth musician Colin Casson takes the reader from Westminster Abbey to Northern Ireland, Europe, Australia – and the Hollywood of the 1950s. Illustrated with more than 60 photographs and filled with amusing anecdotes – including how he came to record the theme tune for The Bridge Over the River Kwai – this entertaining story will strike a chord with musicians everywhere.

978 0 7524 4719 3

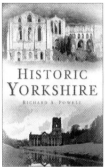

Historic Yorkshire
RICHARD A. POWELL

Including subjects as diverse as Roman Yorkshire, Yorkshire castles and abbeys, historic York and coaching days in Yorkshire, prehistoric Yorkshire, Yorkshire folklore, Robin Hood of Yorkshire, ghost houses, industry, canals and railways, this volume is a fascinating tour through Yorkshire's past. Richly illustrated and meticulously researched, this book will delight all lovers of the Dales.

978 0 7524 4926 5

The Knights Templar in Yorkshire
DIANE HOLLOWAY & TRISH COLTON

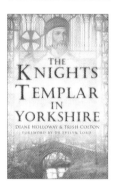

This book explores what life was like during the Templars' stay in Yorkshire. Not only was it the biggest county in Britain, but in Templar terms it was also the richest. They owned more land, property and people in Yorkshire than in any other county in England. This volume takes the reader on an intimate tour of the ten major Templar sites established in Yorkshire, and reveals what life was like for their inhabitants, how the land was farmed, what the population ate, how they were taxed and local legends.

978 0 7509 5087 9

Blind Jack of Knaresborough
ARNOLD KELLET

This is the astonishing story of John Metcalf, otherwise known as Blind Jack of Knaresborough. Written by Dr Arnold Kellett, winner of the Yorkshire Prize for History and an acknowledged expert on the history of the town, it will delight, move and inspire in equal measure.

978 0 7524 4658 5

Visit our website and discover thousands of other History Press books.

www.thehistorypress.co.uk